You-Turn

You-Turn

Saving Our Nation and Ourselves

LYNNE AVERY

WESTBOW
PRESS

A DIVISION OF THOMAS NELSON

WestBow Press books may be ordered through booksellers or by contacting:

WestBow Press
A Division of Thomas Nelson
1663 Liberty Drive
Bloomington, IN 47403
www.westbowpress.com
1-(866) 928-1240

ISBN: 978-1-4497-1758-2 (e)
ISBN: 978-1-4497-1756-8 (sc)
ISBN: 978-1-4497-1757-5 (hc)

Library of Congress Control Number: 2011929104

Printed in the United States of America

WestBow Press rev. date: 6/27/2011

TO MY MOTHER AND FATHER

TO MY SON AND ALL YOUNG PEOPLE
With God's help, the burden will be light

TO GLORIA
My friend

TO PAL
Thanks

CONTENTS

Part IV – The Young: Our Hope for the Future

Part V – Bondage

Part VI – The Power in Truth, Selfless Love and Knowing God

INTRODUCTION

The following description of the rise and fall of the most outstanding civilizations in history should be posted in every classroom, place of employment and government office in our great but struggling nation:

> *The average age of the world's greatest civilizations from the beginning of history, has been about 200 years. During those 200 years, those nations always progressed through the following sequence: The people go from bondage to spiritual truth, from spiritual truth to great courage, from courage to liberty, from liberty to abundance, from abundance to selfishness, from selfishness to apathy, from apathy to dependence, from dependence back again to bondage.*
>
> (Alexander F. Tytler, history professor, University of Edinburgh, Scotland, ***Cycle of Democracy***. 1770)

The United States was a very young country when Professor Tytler made this observation, and our future was still unknown. Over the ensuing 240 years, we have pretty well stuck to the pattern outlined by Dr. Tytler. It isn't hard to see where our country stands in this sequence: one foot in *dependence* and the other in *bondage*.

It would be a mistake for us to think that we cannot lose our freedoms when it has happened to others again and again throughout history. A nation whose people do not routinely practice honesty and fairness and who do not feel connected to each other can easily fall into anarchy during a severe economic depression, when government safety nets become depleted. If we continue to act like vultures, fighting over the carcass of a beached whale called the United States, we may all find ourselves sitting on top of a well- picked skeleton and asking ourselves, "What happened?"

When we look at both the problems that we face, how they developed and even more importantly, why we have been ineffective in solving them, one root cause emerges. That cause is referred to in a little-known verse in the patriotic song "America the Beautiful":

> America! America!
> God shed his grace on thee
> Till selfish gain no longer stain
> The banner of the free!
>
> Katherine Bates

It is interesting to note that Dr. Tytler's sequential model identifies "selfishness" as the entity that begins the decline of great civilizations. For the past half-century our country has increasingly embraced selfish gain, and we are paying the price in every area of our society. I am not talking about profit or gain; that is a normal part of capitalistic interaction. Our country was far more capitalistic and far less selfish fifty years ago than it is today. Rather, I am talking about gain of any kind to which we are not entitled.

One type of gain that we are not entitled to is gain that is itself immoral, such as the gain of another person's husband. Another type of gain that we should reject is gain obtained by the wrong means, such as gain achieved by dishonest or unethical business practices.

When we baby boomers were growing up in the 1950s, our society promoted and honored the Golden Rule. Although we did not always "do unto others as we would have them do unto us", most people were aware that this was the standard society had set and therefore people generally attempted to fulfill that standard much of the time.

Of course, the racial and gender inequalities back in the 1950s were a glaring exception to this. Thankfully, we have made significant headway in addressing those inequities over the past fifty years. Hopefully we will continue to make headway in breaking down the racial and gender walls in our society.

At the beginning of this book, we will revisit life in the United States in the 1950s and early '60s. I suspect many readers will relate to some of the personal anecdotal remembrances. Life was not perfect in the 50s, but kids were safer and freer than they are today. Many of us boomers have forgotten how much freedom we had as kids. We were also more trusting of our fellow citizens and often happier with our personal lives than many children seem to be today. Hopefully tracing the breadcrumbs backward to a place in time when people were less "me"-oriented will remind the baby boomers that we are actually happier when we give more and take less.

More importantly, I hope that a review of life in this country over a half century ago will help the younger readers understand that they are not doomed to live self-centered lives in a self-centered nation. My personal relationships with many young people tell me that this generation desperately needs to hear the message that they are loved unconditionally and that their value has nothing to do with how they look, how much money they have, or what others think of them. Giving to and living for others is what builds the self-esteem that the young today seem to lack.

Next we will put on our tie-dyed shirts and bell-bottomed pants and venture into the late '60s and early '70s to see how and why our nation's values changed. I, like many of my generation, was in the vortex of the 1960s storm and so am able to present many eyewitness accounts of those turbulent times.

Then we will return to the present day and evaluate the problems we face as a society and as individuals in the light of this new value system. Finally, we will consider how we, as individuals, can reverse the downward spiral of our nation and hopefully retain the freedoms that our forefathers fought so hard for. To do this we must unite as a people.

The need for Americans to come together as one people and to work and sacrifice for each other is not just a "nice idea." It is critical to the survival of our democracy. Selfishness leads to conflict and misunderstandings, which opens the door to more laws and less freedom. If we are to avoid the "bondage" that Tytler refers to, all of those who love the United States of America, despite her flaws, must make a personal *you-turn* away from the selfishness that divides us.

When we begin paying forward the Golden Rule, instead of selfishness, the resulting trust, honesty, and unity will enable us to work together and make the most of all of our people's talents and resources as we attempt to solve the problems of this nation. For those who do not love this country or who feel disconnected from her legacy of freedom and opportunity, remember, we are all sitting in a life raft in a rough ocean. Although you may not like the brand of the raft, it would be wise to commit yourself and your oar to rowing with the rest of us toward a safe landfall. Perhaps you will find a connection and love for our nation and its diverse people while working in harmony with the rest of us toward a better future.

DISCLAIMER:
LIFE DOES NOT HAVE A RESET BUTTON

My son once told me that one of his professors described conservatives as people who can't adjust to the present and want to live in the past. Let me assure the reader that neither the title of this book nor its favorable references to years gone by reflect a wish on the author's part to live in the past. First, this is that not possible and second, it is not desirable. It is not possible because we are always moving and changing. We are never standing still. Despite the perception that "history repeats itself," we can never return to the exact same scenario in time. That is one reason that it is so hard to "learn" from history.

Even if we could get in a DeLorean, like Marty McFly, and return permanently to the past, it is not desirable that we do so. There are many things that I suspect most of us would wish to change about the 1950s and early '60s. Many people are rightly ashamed of the racial and gender discrimination that existed back then. These attitudes were destructive to both the dominant and the subservient parties in our nation.

However, even within the most racially oppressed communities, most parents in the '50s were teaching their kids the Golden Rule and all the values associated with it, such as honesty, kindness, and humility. Families across all racial and socio-economic groups were generally intact and one or both of the parents were working. Love and respect were taught in these homes, just like in other households thorough out the nation.

When I was growing up, women were often at home bringing up the kids, and for the kids, that was good. My mom was home every lunch hour and every day after school during my grammar school years. Eventually, some of these moms, including mine, went to work. I was about fifteen by the time my mother entered the work force. The child-rearing years were over and my mom was looking for something to do. She enjoyed her job but I never heard her bemoan the years she spent at home as a mom. I'm sure there were times when she was frustrated, tired and even resentful; however, I don't believe she ever seriously considered just doing what made her feel good while ignoring the responsible things required of a parent.

Undeniably, there are many areas of life that have improved since I was a child. Among many others, the progress in medicine, entertainment, access to information and travel come to mind. However, this progress has been accompanied by an increasingly self-centered value system. This selfishness has caused the loneliness and emptiness that have prevented us from fully utilizing and enjoying the technological and scientific discoveries that we have made over the past fifty years.

I totally realize and freely admit that our nation was not perfect when I was a child. However, government worked, private enterprise thrived, problems got solved, people felt safe and we had more freedom because most people voluntarily submitted themselves to the common good. Perhaps most important of all was that, in general, people liked, trusted, and helped each other. For some, this may have been true only within ethnic groups. However, in general, people still had more interpersonal support even within those groups than many have today.

With the legal and personal commitment to fairness that the past fifty years has brought in our country, we could have a nation whose people are a shining example to the world. But first we must return to the faith, ethical values and individual accountability that founded and has for almost 250 years sustained us as one nation.

PART I

...It Was What It Was

CHAPTER 1

Heroes and Wise Sayings of the '50s

Whether they were cowboys, policemen or super humans, the 1950s childhood television heroes were honest, brave, self-sacrificing, loyal and kind. They played fair and risked all for the common good. Those that carried guns did not shoot first, they did not shoot those who weren't armed and they did not shoot people in the back. Those that fought with fists did not fight dirty, nor did they gang up on a lone opponent. They could be counted on to protect the weak and the defenseless. We kids always knew that no matter what the cost, our heroes would pay it, or at least risk it, to do the right thing. Perhaps our heroes were a little too perfect; however, they set the bar high and so we kids tried a little harder to measure up to that bar.

Even our real life heroes were bigger than life. The press didn't reveal the details of personal failings as they do today, so we kids put Mickey Mantle, John Wayne and President Eisenhower on a pedestal. If information had reached our ears that they had done things that violated their hero status, we would have quickly taken any one of them off that pedestal. Character and respect went hand in hand back then, unlike today, where we often admire and support people's talents and achievements regardless of how profane their characters.

What was life like in the United States in the 1950s and early '60s? Some say that it was a paradise, although somewhat boring. Others say the people themselves were no different than people are today. The latter insist that although it appears that people were generally more honest, fair or patriotic than people are today, in reality, people back then were just better at hiding the same dirty little secrets in their lives that people today don't' bother to hide.

I was born in 1951, at the peak of the baby boomer births, and so am qualified to give an eyewitness testimony to what life was like in the last half of the 1950s and the first half of the '60s. Of course, values and behavior varied from place to place and person to person, however, there was a common set of principles that were promoted and affirmed throughout the country. In addition to looking at the attributes of the heroes of the day, a good way to discern what the values were of a particular place and period in time is to look at the messages in the popular colloquialisms of the day.

Some colloquialisms or common "wise sayings" that I grew up with are listed below. They are organized in categories which reflect the most important issues of the day. These wise sayings were known and respected by almost all of the kids I knew and were frequently heard on television, as well as in our homes and schools:

1. Consequences: *what goes around comes around; you get out of life what you put into it; you reap what you sow; practice what you preach;* and *people in glass houses shouldn't throw stones.* These little admonitions were used often and there was little doubt in my mind that sooner or later, things would be evened up, i.e., justice would be done.

2. Substance over Image: *you can't tell a book by its cover; pretty is as pretty does; you can't make a silk purse out of a sow's ear.* A good one under this topic today might be *a million Christmas lights does not a Christmas make.*

3. Humility: *pride goeth before the fall; you aren't the only pebble on the beach; don't toot your own horn;* and *don't get too big for your britches.* My dad even had a favorite little ditty he used to recite when he felt I or one of my siblings was getting a little too "cocky." It went:

Smarty, Smarty gave a party,
Nobody came but Smarty, Smarty.

4. **Ethics /Friendship:** *a friend in need is a friend indeed; it is better to give than receive; it's the principle of the thing; honesty is the best policy; it's not whether you win or lose, it's how you play the game,* and the one that covers them all, *do unto others as you would have them do unto you.*

CHAPTER 2

The Hollywood Evidence

The entertainment industry, like our heroes and wise sayings, also reflects and validates the value system of a place in time. *The Andy Griffith Show,* a popular 50s television show, was a perfect example not of actual reality but of the values that society had agreed upon in the 1950s.

This show, as with most television shows in the 50s and early '60s, such as *Bonanza, Fury,* and *Gunsmoke,* was not trying to propose that people did not make mistakes as much as they were setting the bar high and role modeling positive behaviors.

Above all, the people in this sitcom were good to one another despite their petty feuds. Mean-spirited behaviors and attitudes such as dishonesty, jealousy, and selfishness were shown to be detrimental to relationships. Further, the negative social consequences of these bad attitudes were almost always revealed during the show and the bad behavior was condemned and corrected.

One of the positive behaviors or attitudes was a tolerance for each other's weaknesses. The characters on this show choose to minimize rather than broadcast and make cruel jokes about the shortcomings of other characters. Barney Fife, the skinny, insecure deputy on *The Andy Griffith Show,* was perhaps one of the weakest and least self-confident characters ever created.

There is an episode that I recall where Barney is convinced that a stranger in town is actually a criminal. He makes an idiot out of himself attempting to catch the suspect committing a crime. Meanwhile, Andy himself notices that Barney's suspect is acting strange, so Andy stakes him out. When Andy sees the suspect attempting to rob the bank, he maneuvers Barney into a position to catch the thief and therefore to redeem his reputation. Andy is happy to watch Barney get the glory, as Barney undoubtedly needed it the most.

Isn't this acceptance of who we are, warts and all, what we all want from a friend, and isn't this why people still love to watch that simple show about people who care for and value one another, despite their shortcomings?

CHAPTER 3

From Father Knows Best
to Father Knows Nothing

The entertainment industry pretty much endorsed the Ten Commandments and especially the golden rule up until the mid-1960s, when little by little, behaviors like dishonesty, cruelty and selfishness began to creep into television shows and movies without condemnation. *All in the Family*, a sitcom about a blue collar family set in the 60s, arrived on the television in 1971.

We didn't know it at the time, but this show and those which followed it over the next half century, would introduce a new standard of behavior. Unlike most prior family shows, the dialogue between characters on *All in the Family* was frequently harsh and negative and the worst side of human nature was often displayed. The laugh lines consisted of a succession of one-line put downs and name-calling between the characters. Instead of trying to bolster the self esteem of the other characters, these characters targeted each other's weaknesses for ridicule.

At first, *All in the Family* and shows that imitated it used satire to expose racism, sexism and general bad attitudes. As time went on, there was less and less condemnation of the selfishness, dishonesty, cruelty, and bad manners. Eventually the negative behaviors became normalized and were presented in a morally neutral way. Today's televisions sitcoms commonly portray callous acts and harsh words even between friends and family members. Whatever good these shows have accomplished on the issue of racial and gender inequality has been offset by these negative social trends that they have helped to establish and reinforce.

I admit that my childhood experience was not as simple as the episodes on *Father Knows Best*. Obviously, any show that has to present, solve and wrap up a significant life problem in 22 minutes, as *Father Knows Best* did, is going to have to make some serious compromises when it comes to representing reality. However, the family relationships in that sitcom, with their mutual affection, respect and parental honesty, were consistent with the parent/child relationships I observed while growing up.

Conversely, I never witnessed the social ignorance or the sustained verbal abuse and disrespect among family members, as portrayed in *All in the Family, The Simpsons* or the many others of that ilk that have followed. Proponents of these shows have stated that they believe that they are doing society a favor by alerting the denser ones among us to the reality of human imperfection. It might come as a surprise to the media moguls that the fact that people aren't perfect isn't a news flash.

Many of these new sitcoms do not just show the normal weaknesses and strengths in human beings. Rather they seem to delight in showing over and over again how overwhelmingly pathetic they believe adults to be. Prior to the late 1960s, fathers had been portrayed as the source of most wisdom and authority in our families. Maybe that's why they became the target of the bulk of the degrading humor on the new shows.

It is often said that the characters in the television shows of the 50s were one-dimensional. However, the same could be said for these newer characters that are often mere caricatures of racists or sexists or some other politically incorrect figure. Truly, these new shows ended up presenting stereotypical characters and behavior just as much as the shows they replaced.

When this new genre of sitcoms such as *All in the Family* and later *The Simpsons* arrived on the scene there was a public discussion as to whether these new types of "tell it like it is" family situations were more realistic than the old *traditional, competent parents in charge* sitcoms like *Leave It to Beaver* and *Father Knows Best.* The allegation wasn't just that people had changed. It was that we had always been more like Homer Simpson or Archie Bunker than like Andy Griffith. The media's spin has asserted that the newer shows are more "realistic" because they show the "true" flaws and deviance that we all supposedly harbor and have always harbored in our minds and hearts. The following excerpts from an article written by Eliezer Van Allen (Stanford University, March 12, 2000) called *The Simpsons: An Imperfect Ideal Family* take this exact position:

Unlike common representations of the "typical" American family seen in television shows like "Father Knows Best" or "Leave It to Beaver", "The Simpsons" presents a family unit that is all at once unique, attainable, and lovable, unlike those presented in either of the other two shows. From the show's creators' rebellion against "traditional" family sitcoms to each of the Simpson family member's caricatures, this show satirizes, but ultimately redeems, each unit of the nuclear family (father, mother, and children) [1]. The Simpsons may actually reflect the way many families actually live, for better or worse, and is thus culturally pivotal towards guiding the American nuclear family into the future."

The statement that *The Simpsons...are all at once unique, attainable and loveable, unlike those (characters) presented in Father Knows Best or Leave it to Beaver* is absurd. I can agree that the Simpsons, with their low effort and achievement levels are easily "obtainable", and perhaps amusing, but loveable? Pathetic, ignorant and irritating are more accurate adjectives. Who would want Bart Simpson for a son or Homer for a dad?

It was perhaps predictable that after a long period of time when society presented life as a little too squeaky clean, our society would be receptive to entertainment that portrayed life as less black and white and more grey. Unfortunately, as we shall see, we over reacted and ended up eliminating many ethical values such as honesty, kindness, and fairness in our entertainment and replacing them with endorsements of dishonesty, cruelty, and selfishness.

It is too bad that so many of today's younger generation have come to accept as normal the self- centered mentality that dominates our culture today. Not long ago, my son had me watch part of a popular show that featured plastic surgeons. One surgeon demanded that a patient of his wear a bag over her head while he had sex with her because, to him, she was still so unattractive. The *appearance challenged* girl was scheduled for several more surgeries to hopefully get her to the point where she could face people without shame. When I heard the dialogue, I thought it was a joke. It wasn't. It is no surprise that so many young people's self-esteem in our society is dependent on their personal appearance.

Many in Hollywood have denied responsibility for our debased cultural trends. They insist that they are merely presenting life as it is. The relationship between entertainment and cultural trends is a little more complicated than that. It is more of a lead-and-follow and follow-and-lead dance on both sides. Many of our young people imitate what they see coming out of Hollywood and in return, Hollywood continues to pump out films and television shows glorifying characters that lack even basic empathy or decency.

As already stated, it is especially critical that the under age thirty-five group, on whose shoulders our nation's problems will soon come to rest, learn to care about, trust and understand each other. Otherwise, how will they ever be able to work effectively together toward solving our problems? Sadly, many young people believe that the "get what you can for yourself" mentality is normal and is the way it has always been. Regardless of the flaws in their arguments, articles like the one by Mr. Van Allen solidified the message that *Father Knows Best* was a sanitized, goodie-two-shoes version of life in America in the 50s that never really existed.

The revisionist lie is that behind our closed doors and shuttered windows, we have always been an ill-mannered, bad-mouthed, child-molesting, adulterous, racist, sexist, selfish, dishonest people. One reason that this viewpoint is popular is that it makes the current moral vacuum in our society more palatable. It also diminishes, in the minds of the young, the possibility that things can be different. Unfortunately for the revisionists, there are still living witnesses like myself who know the truth. No, *Father Knows Best* did not exist in all of its purity and perfection. However, there was a time not long ago when people were far more honest, generous, equitable and trustworthy.

So, let's put on our ked sneakers and white socks and get into our DeLorean and take a little trip back to the 1950s and early '60s. We will find a world without computers and a time when the televisions had three channels. Just as shocking, we will find a time when most people still believed that *honesty is the best policy, you get out of life what you put into it...it is more blessed to give than to receive,* and *it isn't whether you win or lose, it's how you play the game.*

PART II

The Nation of My Childhood

CHAPTER 4

If the Mitten Doesn't Fit...

On a winter's day in 1957, I went to my school's "lost and found" and discovered a pair of mittens that suited my taste and fit perfectly. I told the office clerk that they were mine and happily walked out. Later that day, on the playground, a boy came up to me, pointed at the mittens and said, "Those are mine." I denied that possibility and we ended up in the principal's office, each telling our opposing stories without the benefit of an attorney.

The famous words "if the mitten doesn't fit, you must acquit" had not yet been spoken, and so an hour later the rightful owner of the mittens and I were both still sitting in the principal's office while the school administrators waited to see which one of us six-year-olds would "crack" first.

As time passed, I grew weary of my captivity and began to contemplate what life would be like growing up in my school's office. How much longer would this boy hold out? A glance at my accuser's face told me that he would outlast me because his expression radiated something that I would later come to identify as *righteous anger*.

Sometime between the first and second hours of my ordeal, my six-year-old resolve collapsed and I confessed that I had never laid eyes on those mittens before that morning when I had engaged in a little "lost and found" browsing.

My parents were notified that I had stolen another child's property and had then lied about it. The consequences were swift and, I have to assume, severe, as that part of the story has been deleted from my memory banks. It was more than a year later before I found myself back in the principal's office for taking a stuffed monkey named "Zippy" from another kid's locker and showing it for "show and tell" as my own. What can I say? I was a slow learner. Besides, I had a small obsession with zippy monkeys, as will be seen in another story. That time, I realized resistance was only postponing the inevitable, so I confessed in the hallway on my way to the office.

I only recall one subsequent "lesson" during my childhood on the subject of theft and dishonesty. It was an isolated incident that occurred when I was about seven. It seems that I was confused about my obligation to take money out versus put money into the Sunday school collection plate, or at least that is the story I stuck to. I will always remember the humiliation I felt when my parents made me give those quarters back to the Sunday school teacher.

Although these incidents occurred over half a century ago, I can still feel the shame when I remember my bad behavior. One of the many lessons that I learned early was that adults put a high value on honesty, and eventually, I did too.

CHAPTER 5

The Golden Rule

I grew up in a small Midwestern college town on the flat prairie lands of Illinois, surrounded by alfalfa, soybeans and corn fields. As are most small-to-midsize college towns, my hometown was sometimes an uneasy marriage between academia and the real world of small family businesses, farmers, and blue collar workers. Overall, it was a good mix. The open-minded, forward-looking vision of the university element was tempered by the strong traditional value system of the town and vice-versa.

I realize that not everyone in the U.S. in the '50s and '60s was living in a place with the traditional values of a Midwestern college town. However, as already discussed, the mass media and entertainment industry, as well as the popular sayings and heroes of that time, indicate that the entire nation was promoting a basic standard of good behavior--the Golden Rule.

The Golden Rule is sometimes called the *ethics of reciprocity* because it tells us to *do unto others as we would have them do unto us* or to *love our neighbor as ourselves*. This principle was role modeled continually in the movies, books and television programs of the '50s. The theme of solving problems by attempting to do what was fair was reinforced everywhere, including at school, at home, on sports teams and at church. Most kids in my neighborhood went to church with their family from a young age, and there they heard and believed the Bible teachings about love, honesty, kindness and the Golden Rule.

Whenever the golden rule or the issues included in the *Ten Commandments* were discussed or challenged, people in the '50s generally pointed to the *Bible* as the ultimate authority on the importance of living by those guidelines. The observation that "God says" that we are to tell the truth, be generous or play fair was usually the statement that ended the discussion, as we had not yet as a society begun to argue with God's wisdom.

When we attempt to live by the standard of "doing unto others as we would have them do unto us," it infiltrates every area of life and directs every decision. When we look at life and its choices through the glasses of the golden rule, we find that our choices are limited to the virtues that implement that rule. Throughout this book, we will discuss these virtues, such as honesty, personal responsibility, patience, humility, generosity, fairness, forgiveness, repentance, integrity and reverence.

If the golden rule is to come alive in our lives, it must be more than words. It must be revealed in our choices to live out these virtues. To the degree that a society practices these things, we have freedom, safety, hope, peace of mind and prosperity. Shortly, we will see how these virtues were manifest in our nation when we baby boomers were kids.

But first I want to recognize and pay my respects to the ones that set and met, to the best of their ability, the standard of the golden rule in the 1950s: the baby boomers' parents, the WWII generation. They are often called "the greatest generation," although it is consistent with the humility of that generation that it was not they who gave themselves that lofty label.

---------------------------------- CHAPTER 6 ----------------------------------

Parents Were "Adults"

Just as it is today, in the '50s there were excellent, average and not-so-great dads and moms. Even though every parent was different, as a generation, the post-WWII parents of the baby boomers had a style of parenting that was distinctive to their generation. So who were these parents and how did they maintain discipline and respect in families with an average of three to five kids per household?

The first thing they were was "The Parents." Unlike today, the '50s parents were rarely their kids' "buddies" and they were generally not as much fun for kids to hang out with as parents are now. They did not feel obligated to adopt our clothing styles, attempt to appreciate our music or learn the names of our generational heroes.

Back then, parents and kids lived in two different worlds. The parents were "up there" and we kids were down below. The power and privileges were in their world, but so were the responsibilities. Therefore, our parents were also our greatest protectors, role models and character molders. As strange as it may seem to kids today, my parents' generation did not care so much if their children really liked them, although I'm sure they loved us and wanted us to love them. First and foremost, they were committed to keeping us safe and raising us to be productive, decent, and law-abiding citizens.

The following five common characteristics of my parents and their generation demonstrate the maturity and responsibility that they displayed, even when they were still in their early 20s, as they handled the adult issues of life.

1. Parents were adults: When I was growing up, most parents grew up and became adults. They did this at various ages, depending on their circumstances. They accepted responsibility and lived up to the requirements dictated by their own actions, including the act of becoming parents. Many '50s parents had their first child in their late teens or early 20s and would chronologically be considered kids today. They had nothing in common with the sitcom parents of today, with their silliness and irresponsibility. Back then, immaturity and acting like children at thirty was not considered to be an admirable trait or behavior pattern.

When I was born, my parents lived in a New England state where birth control was illegal. My grandfather's best friend, an M.D., kindly provided my mother with an illegal and what proved to be a very defective diaphragm. I and my three siblings had arrived, no more than one and a half years apart, by the time my parents were twenty-three.

If we were to pick from the pool of twenty-three year olds today, I believe we would have a hard time finding two of them that, after becoming the parents of four unplanned children within four years, would or could complete their educations without accepting a dollar of public assistance. In addition to achieving financial independence, my parents went on to fulfill their responsibilities as spouses, parents, employees and citizens for fifty-plus years, with little complaint. It may seem impossible that just two generations ago people were taking on full adult responsibilities at an age when many of today's youth are still living like kids in their parents' homes.

Today the government has stepped in and, via entitlement programs, become the provider in many families who started out like mine did. The fathers are forced out of the homes so the mothers can qualify for welfare. What a different life I would have led with the government as my father.

One of the benefits of parents being adults was that we children were rarely included in family decision making. We were not even consulted on the brand of cereal or soda our moms bought at the store, and we were often told outright that certain things were "none of our business." Growing up, I sometimes wished I had more power over my life but I now realize that more power goes hand in hand with responsibility and stress. Because we weren't forced to deal with inappropriate adult issues and because our parents did, we were free to be kids and to wrestle with and learn from appropriate kid-level problems.

In fact, it was a dangerous thing to meddle in the affairs of adults when I was a kid, as I learned when I was about eight or nine. One morning, I overheard my parents discussing a neighbor who was also a skater on the speed skating team our family belonged to. My parents were unhappy because this skater was selling the fund raiser candy two days before the official kick-off date. This handicapped the other sellers who waited for the official start date.

I took it upon myself to go to the errant skater's house and inform her parents of my parent's sentiments. In one seamless chain of events, the chastised parents made a phone call to mine, the front door opened on my house and a whistle blew for you–know–who.

I ran home as *fast as my little legs would carry me*, as that was the message coded in that whistle. I was greeted on the porch by two angry parents with their hands on their hips. After what seemed like several hours of lecturing on the evils of meddling in "adult business," the sin of "eavesdropping," and the family rule of "what is said in the house stays in the house," I was sent to my room for the duration of the day. Looking back, it seems as though I was in trouble a significant amount of my childhood days. There was a lot to learn, and my folks intended that I learn it all.

2. Parents were clear in expectations and consistent in consequences-Most parents in real life and on television in the '50s were consistent in enforcing the household rules. These rules were clearly delineated. Adults in the '50s rarely allowed their mood, their physical health or the circumstances surrounding an infraction to change their dedication to enforcing the well-publicized rules and values that they expected their children to live by. They did exactly what they said they were going to do, when they were going to do it, for good or for bad. They also approved of or disapproved of the same behaviors day after day.

Teachers, our friends' parents, neighbors, police, businesses owners and employers all operated with a level of consistency that is rarely seen today. As we used to say in referring to the consequences adults would attach to certain unwanted behavior, you could "count on it" or "set your clock by it." There is much to be said for knowing exactly what the punishment will be before one commits a forbidden act. This left very little "wiggle room" for kids' bad behavior. In other words, we kids rarely wasted our breath on excuses. In my household, kids offering excuses for bad behavior tended to make my parents' mood even darker.

I can remember many occasions when I had what I considered a perfectly legitimate excuse that I didn't even bother to offer up, as I knew very well that it would not mitigate the punishment. Many times in my young life, I wished that my parents would let me off the hook for doing what I knew was wrong. They had a much different outlook than many parents today. From their point of view, as this next story shows, certain behaviors were inexcusable, period, end of story.

I recall the day that I was in second or third grade math class and was about to give my math paper to the student next to me for grading. At that moment, the teacher spoke: *"If the paper you receive to grade does not have a name on it, please place a '0' on it and return it to its owner."*

Having retained physical control over my nameless math paper, I picked up my pen and began to write my name on it. The hyper-vigilant girl who was waiting to grade my paper then grabbed it off my desk and took it to the teacher to be marked "0" credit because I had not written my name on it (thanks to *Miss Butzkeyinski*.) So, being a little upset with this goodie-two-shoes and my declining math grade, I waited for her after school and administered a very small amount of "street justice."

As noted earlier, my parents, as did most of their peers, believed that certain things were right all of the time and certain things were wrong all of the time. Hence, since fighting was wrong, except when it was a case of self defense, it was useless to tell my parents about the incident at school which had provoked the attack. I accepted my punishment and kept quiet about the provocation which, to this day, I believe was significant.

It may seem to today's younger generations that my parents' generation was overly rigid, legalistic, and even boring, and at times, they were. Today, parents may be more understanding and more flexible, but this understanding and flexibility have sometimes prevented enforcing necessary limits and have undermined the teaching of absolute right and wrong. Too much flexibility can also compromise the necessary hierarchy of the parent/child relationship by making it difficult for parents to retain authority.

My parent's consistency is what gave them credibility. They did not talk a good talk one day and then ignore the very behavior they had condemned the next day. So many parents today act like children ourselves, as our values blow with the wind and our kids learn to disrespect us.

3. They practiced what they preached- Adults set and usually met the bar when I was growing up. Most adults during my childhood understood that their kids were not just listening to what they said but were watching what they did. My parents recognized the foolishness, not to mention the hypocrisy, in the idea that children will "do as I say and not as I do."

They therefore mostly "practiced what they preached." They preached fairness and the golden rule and they were usually fair in their interactions with their friends, family, business involvements and even with strangers. They preached honesty, reliability, hard work and modesty and they were all of these things almost all of the time.

4. **Parents in the '50s were more concerned with substance than image:** The '50s were undoubtedly a time of few words and more action when it came to parenting. Parents back then did not hug their kids as much, rarely told us that they loved us, and almost never bragged about us. They did, however, make their marriages work, kept us safe, provided for us and taught us right from wrong.

Today, we tend to hug our kids and tell them we love them a lot and then, too often, we do things that are detrimental to them. For instance, many parents today allow our children to play video games, talk on computer social networks or skateboard rather than do their homework. Then we act surprised at the child's inevitable failure in school.

Today parents frequently allow our kids to go to places and do things that are not safe or good for them. Peer pressure meant almost nothing to parents in the '50s, who were more concerned with the issues of safety, obedience and decency. If an event was not safe and decent, we were not allowed to go and it didn't matter if the President of the United States himself were attending, we would not be.

5. **They were hard workers and self-starters-** Adults in the '50s were generally hard workers and resisted accepting financial aid or help from neighbors or the government. The expression "God helps those who help themselves" was tightly adhered to. My parents' generation believed and proved that "you get out of life what you put into it." The passage of time has shown that this philosophy served the WWII generation well. It is no accident that many in their generation learned to play highly demanding and complex games such as bridge and chess, for fun, and mastered musical instruments with a nonchalance that often appeared effortless.

The WWII generation was and is independent in their actions and beliefs, relative to subsequent generations. When I was a kid, parents set their own standards and were rarely swayed by the new trends or by what was going on in the neighbor's house. They also needed a minimum of supervision on jobs or to get things done at home. There was little need for the surveillance cameras, and phone and computer monitors that we have today.

Now, as only a remnant of this unique generation lingers on in their twilight years, this work ethic and determination to meet life head-on is still evident. One of their stronghold communities is Sun City, Arizona. This city of 40,000+ is as neat as a pin, and it is common to see octogenarians working in their yards, keeping up their "pride of ownership."

This city is dubbed "the city of volunteers" for good reason. Everywhere one looks, these elderly citizens are giving of their time, money and/ or talents to make the community a better place to live. They serve on condo associations; provide security, volunteer for community bands and work on clean-up crews. A large number of volunteers are involved with the Sun City "posse" and provide year-round surveillance to prevent crime, as well as assistance for elderly shut-ins. Whether it is the posse or proactive concerned neighbors, these people take care of one another.

Truly, the energy levels, selflessness and interconnectedness that are on display in that senior city are a tribute to the WWII generation's undying commitment to live each day fully, to the very last one. An observer of this community would quickly see that these elderly citizens, with the vast majority of their days behind them, still face life with more optimism and interest than many younger and healthier individuals. The personal responsibility has given them a "can do "attitude and their faith and values has directed their choices as to what they "should do."

For those who doubt that this portrayal of the WWII generation is accurate, take a moment and look at a few obituaries. Many members of this "greatest generation" came back from the war, got their educations, made great careers, raised families, then retired and then went on to be as busy and productive in their retirement years as in the prior 60.

If I were to pinpoint the characteristics that best describe the strength of my parents' generation, it would be responsibility without excuses and a non-negotiable value system based on the Golden Rule. When there was a moral principle involved, adults in the 1950s tended to ask themselves, "What is the right thing to do?" and then they just did it. They did not cloud the issue or torment themselves by weighing what was a moral choice in terms of personal profit or loss.

Their volunteerism, honesty and neighborliness were not forced upon these WWII survivors by the government, nor has it been necessary to shame them into this behavior with media campaigns. They do it of their own free will and because of who they are. That is what makes it so valuable.

We baby boomers had an expression in the '60s: "Just do it." Actually, it was really my mom and dad's generation that "just did it" long before excuses, rationalizations and justifications replaced apologies, confessions and just doing the right thing to begin with.

So here's to my parents, the authoritative molders of my character and guardians of my formative years. And here's to millions more like them all across this great land who did their best to pass their faith and guiding principles on to the next generation.

Now let's take a look at some of those guiding principles and the impact they had on me and my generation's childhood world.

CHAPTER 7

Honesty Was the Policy

Honesty is a virtue that was practiced throughout the nation when I was growing up. Honesty is critical to the survival of a friendship, marriage, family or a democratic society and, it is practiced less and less today.

As the prior story about the mittens shows, honesty was a high priority for adults and for our society in the '50s. It was so important that we kids were often punished more for lying than we were for the crime we were lying about. All the kids I knew were familiar with the story of how our first president, George Washington, cut down a valuable cherry tree when he was only a boy. The story goes that young George avoided punishment because he told his father the truth about what he'd done. Unfortunately, my parents were not as charitable as George's dad and a full confession rarely resulted in a full pardon. They expected their kids to be honest and so they didn't see any reason to reward it.

Honesty is a virtue that must be practiced if we are to live by the Golden Rule. We are told in the Bible that Satan is the "father of lies" and that His greatest power comes from deceit. (John 8:4, NIV) When we lie, we join forces with evil and help it to prosper. We are far freer to commit shameful acts when we plan to hide our behavior afterwards by lying.

Many, if not most, adults that I knew in the '50s never told a lie that I know of. Despite money problems, my parents did not lie about how many people were in our car going in a drive-in theater or how many were in the family when staying in a motel. They did not take pens, paper or any supplies from their places of employment and, if a cashier handed my mom or dad too much change, they (my parents) gave the additional amount back. When they took matches in a restaurant, they took one pack and they did not take the extra sugar or crackers from the table. They would not have stolen a flea off a dog. The same could be said for my mother- and father-in-law. These examples may seem like petty stuff, but it was "the principle of the thing." If a behavior was right, it was right in the big and the small things.

I know it is hard to imagine for those young people who have only lived in our current world, but most people in the '50s just did not have to worry about theft, vandalism or other types of "dishonest" behavior. The vast majority of the time when someone hit a parked car and couldn't locate the owner, they left a note with their identifying information. Most did this because it was the right thing to do. I know this because these notes would appear even in the night when no one was around to see the accident. My parents would have been furious if they found out that one of us kids had hit a car and not left a note with their insurance company on it. I believe their first comment would have been, "How would you feel if someone did that to you?" Today a more common question would likely be "Did anyone see you do it?"

Theft was almost non-existent in my home town in the '50s. People rarely locked their cars and if they locked their houses at all, they did so only at night or when they went on vacation. Our family hid a house key outside in the same place for fifteen years, and the whole neighborhood knew where it was. During those fifteen years we never had a theft or unwanted guest.

We did not lock our bikes up but laid them on the ground at the store, park, pool, cornfields or wherever we stopped. We left them outside in our unfenced front yards or in our driveways overnight. Those very rare kids that did lock up their bikes were considered strange and paranoid. In fact, I don't remember seeing the stores even selling bike locks until I was a teenager.

In my entire childhood, I never knew a kid whose bike was stolen or an adult whose car was stolen or house broken into. If a kid had been so insane as to take another kid's bike, getting away with the bike would only have been half the problem. It is likely that when the thief brought home the bike of dubious acquisition, his/her parents would have grilled him/her for as long as it took, or "until the cows came home," to get to the truth about where the bike had come from.

These days, parents and other adults in authority frequently overlook dishonesty in our children, even when it is obvious. When two children are telling opposite stories, rather than sweat it out of one or the other, parents or those in authority will often either punish them both or let both off. This sends the message that honesty isn't important. If you send this message too many times when your child is young, you will likely have a child who lies to you all of his or her life.

When I was growing up, I was sure that regardless of the circumstances, adults were going to tell the truth. I was not a perfectly behaved child, and even routine parent-teacher conferences always made me nervous. However, I always knew that whatever any teacher said about me would be the truth, for good or bad. My parents also knew it and, often to my detriment, they never doubted what the teachers said. The result was that justice was often done, problems were solved and we kids usually felt that we had been dealt with fairly, regardless of whether we were guilty of bad behavior or a victim of it.

Why is honesty so important? After all, lies are only words. What harm can they do? If we look closely, we see that lying causes an enormous amount of damage to the fabric of society. It destroys trust and respect, creates confusion about what is real and inhibits solutions by distorting the facts. When we lie to one another, we deceive others and often ourselves about who we are. Love is dependent on trust, respect and the truth. So when we lie, we destroy trust, respect, reality and love.

Today's problems are complex enough. When we add the element of dishonesty, people often become paralyzed, not knowing what to do because we don't know what is true. It is hard enough to decide what the correct solutions to complex problems are, but to have to first determine what "facts" are true makes it almost impossible.

When honesty is practiced in a neighborhood, town or country, it bonds people together. People in the '50s were free to come and go without fear for personal safety, of loss of possessions, or of random attacks on their reputation. Needless to say, our trust and affection for one another was greatly increased when we were not being constantly victimized by others.

CHAPTER 8

Freedom to Choose and Sometimes Lose

Our founding fathers wanted to preserve freedom for all who lived and would live in this land. However, freedom is on the decline here. There are too many people and too many overlapping rights to be as free as we were 100 years ago. Lack of personal accountability also leads to less freedom. We cannot do much about the first reality but we can do something about the second.

The essential partner to freedom is personal accountability. Accountability was very important to parents in the '50s and so they generally expected it from their kids from a young age. We kids were actually told by teachers and parents to "check ourselves" first when things went wrong. Only after we had done that could we scan the horizon for a co-defendant to blame.

We all knew that attempting to blame someone else for the results of a decision in which we had a part would only inflame the situation. Attempting to blame someone else for our own misdemeanors would guarantee an enhanced punishment more surely than anything other than lying. So our minds did not get in the habit of looking for someone other than ourselves to blame. We tended to think more along the lines of "What did I do that caused or allowed this mess and how can I avoid such a mess in the future?"

This strong expectation of personal accountability meant that lawsuits were rare when I was growing up. People who filed lawsuits did so quietly because filing a lawsuit, except in a case of extreme criminal negligence, was considered to be an opportunistic, anti-social act. This has changed, and today, because there are so many lawsuits, we have enacted endless numbers of laws to protect us from ourselves and others and each other's attorneys. These days one can suffer a loss from one's own recklessness and still sue another. Instead of "checking" ourselves first, our minds are now more in the habit of searching for someone else to blame and, if we are lucky, force to pay.

This emphasis on personal responsibility within the context of a law-abiding society, enabled kids in the '50s to be more physically independent from adults than most kids today are allowed to be. We were free to come and go, free to direct many of our own activities, free to roam the city, free to choose who we spent our time with, free to be creative and to push the limits, and free to play just about anywhere there was space.

Beginning at ages eight or nine, my friends, my siblings and I were permitted to ride our bikes all over town in the company of older siblings. Unlike today, our parents were not petrified at the thought of us having free, unsupervised time, nor did they panic when we were out of sight for the entire day. Cell phones were not in existence and using pay phones was extravagant, so we generally waited until we got home to tell our parents about how we had met and solved the problems that came up that day.

In the summertime we would ride our bikes eight to ten miles a day, stopping at a variety of our favorite places. One of our favorite stops was at the university veterinary farm, where a herd of horses was pastured. We would bring our halters and bridles with us and catch and ride the horses bareback. Several of the horses were quite big. A few times one of the onsite veterinarians came over to warn us to "be careful", as initially we were not familiar with the horses' personalities. As negligent as those men's *laissez-faire* attitudes may seem today, it makes the point that, at a time where liability lawsuits were rare, even we children were often given the freedom to choose what risks we would take. We kids were perfectly aware of the dangers of riding horses we didn't know. But we had decided that the risk was worth it.

We also rode our bikes to the community pool, located about six miles away. There, we spent most of our time playing tag and doing flips and exotic dives off the high dive. Sometimes a kid would stand on the lower level of the diving tower and as the jumper flew by on his way down from the high dive, the kid on the lower tower would toss him a ball. Today kids at the age of 12 or so generally must have their parents in the area. Back then the lifeguards watched us. They did a good job, but too many got sued and now parents must be on site.

Sometimes we would go to the school gym, where the bleachers were stacked almost all of the way to the ceiling. We would get the end of the rope that was attached to the ceiling for climbing and carry it to the top of the twenty-five to thirty foot high bleachers, sit down on the rope's knot and jump off. We could swing from one end of the gym to the other. We attempted a similar maneuver with the school flagpole. One kid sat in the rope and the others pushed them around the swaying flagpole. The flexibility of the pole is what gave the ride a whiplash. After about thirty minutes of riding, we discovered that the flagpole was permanently bent. About that time the night janitor arrived and put an end to our fun.

Other times we would go to one of the university barns and jump out of the upstairs door down into the hay below. Once we brought homemade "parachutes" made out of pillowcases. The milk cows in the barn found our antics alarming and responded with moos and kicking. The fact is that kids of every generation often have the best time while pushing the limits of routine activities, such as pulling each other on skateboards behind bikes and riding three on a bike down a hill.

Riding three on a bike is something you almost never see today but was quite common in my neighborhood. Looking back, I'm not sure why we did it, as almost every kid had a bike of (her) own. Personally, I enjoyed the higher vantage point of sitting on the handlebars.

One fine summer day I was riding down a steep hill on the handlebars of my brother's bike. My friend was on the seat and my younger brother, Steve, was standing up in the middle peddling like a maniac. He had little choice in the matter as the brakes were in the pedals and therefore beyond his ability to access in his upright position. We were not wearing helmets (what were they?) and I was not wearing shoes. I had on a pair of thongs. Talk about a cluster of violations of today's safety standards. We were a moving, pending disaster.

Sure enough, as we approached a blind intersection, my high vantage point allowed me to see over the hedges to view a car approaching from the right and destined to intersect our path in a matter of seconds. With no time to alert my brother, I chose to vacate my perch.

Unfortunately, as I was jumping off the handlebars, I stuck my foot into the moving spokes, flipping the bike. We did avoid what would have been a nasty collision; however, I managed to rip off the entire skin pad under my big toe. My foot was bleeding impressively and my ankle was swelling rapidly. My brother and friend were in surprisingly good shape, and I attributed that to my last-minute sacrifice.

My friend, who had once broken a finger, did a quick visual exam and assured me that, based on her (vast) experience with broken bones, my ankle was only sprained. The two uninjured parties decided that it was better for me to limp home rather than risk further irritating my mother, whose disgust at our folly was likely to exceed her pity for my injuries. So the two uninjured ones walked while I hobbled the mile and a half home, where we received the predictable lecture on personal responsibility and using "the brains God gave us."

Summer gave way to fall and school and the time of year to celebrate the big holidays. On Halloween, after gathering up our friends, my brothers and sister and I would go out "Trick or Treating" in our costumes. The younger kids in the neighborhood, ages five or six on up, would join with older brothers and sisters on those dark Halloween nights, as no respectable kids over six would be caught dead trick or treating with their parents.

In those days, every house light was on to greet the kids. Although we were always eager to get on to the next treat at the next house, we patiently waited while the adults tried to guess who we were and marveled at our costumes.

Some neighbors set tables and chairs out so visiting kids could sit and eat homemade donuts and enjoy a glass of apple cider. Some houses had water-filled tubs set up so we could "bob for apples." This was always a saliva-filled adventure for the late comers. We received homemade taffy apples and popcorn balls at some houses and we ate as we went and never had to worry about razor blades or poison. We were free to enjoy a fun holiday with our peers without fear.

If someone had told us kids then that within 10 years or so, kids would be getting their candy x-rayed for razor blades and we would need a "tester" for poison, we would still be laughing. Razor blades and poison, indeed!

Wintertime also provided my friends and I with unfettered opportunities to push our limits and "live and learn." Not long after the last maple and oak leaves had turned colors and fallen to the ground to be raked and burned in bonfires in our own yards, winter would arrive. Regardless of what the calendar said, we knew it was winter when we had our first snowfall.

Video games, the computer and DVDs were not in existence in the '50s, and the three television channels available had 90 percent adult programming. Most of us would have preferred to have had our teeth worked on without Novocain rather than to have been forced to watch an hour of Walter Cronkite. We therefore spent more time playing outside, even in the winter, than most kids do today in any season.

Once outside we would pursue a variety of activities. We built snow forts and stocked them with piles of ammunition. We would, on occasion, make the snowballs into ice balls by watering them and letting them freeze overnight. We learned the hard way how much damage an ice ball can do to a kid's face!

We often went ice skating on a pond thorough which a river ran, and that part of the pond never froze. The city had built a crude warming hut, installed a spotlight and some "beware" signs about skating on open water or thin ice and then washed their hands of it. On a few occasions, those who chose not to "beware" and skated too close to the open water fell through the ice. I don't believe that anyone ever drowned, as the pond was quite shallow, but I suspect that the shock of falling into ice water was a learning experience that made a lasting impression on the victims.

The pond was a challenge in many ways. When the wind driven waters froze it caused the surface of the pond to be bumpy. Aside from the rough texture of the ice, there were foreign objects frozen into the surface that presented dangerous obstacles while skating. The occasional protruding tree limb or, in one instance, a half submerged duck, were obstacles that occasionally caused us to fall head over heels across the ice. At night, when we skated beyond the radiance of the lone light that shined from the warming hut, these obstacles became invisible. Despite these booby traps, most of us kids preferred the frozen pond to the manicured commercial ice at the local ice rink any day.

There was freedom at the pond. We could skate clockwise or spin in circles, whereas counter-clockwise was the only acceptable direction at the ice rink. There were no rink guards at the pond and so we could play "crack the whip," tag or hide–and–seek, or whatever game we could make up. (Crack the whip is a fun game that involves a chain of skaters holding hands while skating and taking tight turns at high speeds. The fun comes upon releasing the person on the end of the "whip" at just the right moment so that the combination of the highest speed and tightest angle assure that the victim will end up sprawled across the ice or lodged in a nearby tree.)

Sometimes we would skate off into the dark, unfamiliar inlets of the pond to look at the bright winter stars. We all knew a few of the constellations and we would identify them over and over again. We didn't know it then, but that freedom to direct our activities without thousands of laws and regulations was like those constellations. In reality, even as we looked at those arrangements of stars, they had already changed, leaving only their trail of light behind. The freedoms we enjoyed were already being undermined. Once again, we had no clue what we had or what we were about to lose. Freedom, for us, was the norm and we gave it as much thought as we did the oxygen in the air.

Whenever we could get a ride, we went to the local sliding hill. We would launch ourselves on our sleds and toboggans down the hill with reckless abandon. We never tired of the thrill of attempting to avoid immoveable objects while traveling at high speeds, only to arrive at a four foot high embankment, which we flew over to land on the hopefully frozen lake. I say "hopefully" because we rarely checked the condition of the lake before the first run. Then we would walk ourselves and our "ride" back up the hill. It is not surprising that childhood obesity was very rare when I was growing up.

One time several of our sleds broke. Those flexible flyers just couldn't handle that landing on the lake after flying over the embankment. A quick search of a nearby dumpster provided us with cardboard boxes, which we opened and laid flat. Then we colored the bottom part with crayons to make them faster. We scrunched ourselves onto the little rectangles and pushed off down the hill. We discovered, much to our delight, that these new "rides" lacked even the illusion of directional control. An added bonus was that their rate of acceleration and top speed were off the charts. As far as we kids were concerned, they offered the ride of a lifetime.

We passed the details of our accidental discovery on to every kid we saw that day. We didn't bother to mention the incidental fact that almost every one of us who had ridden one of those contraptions was bruised, scraped and limping.

People, and especially children, don't always make the best choices. To that, we used to say "live and learn." In the '50s, we kids were often accused of acting like we "didn't have a brain in our heads." The upside to that attitude is that we realized from an early age that we were not victims and that, rather, we often had the power in our own hands to affect outcomes in our lives. We were therefore more likely to use "the brains God gave us" to solve our own problems and thereby direct our own destinies.

There is no doubt that in the '50s some kids were injured or died because of a lack of laws or controls regulating their behavior. Sledding, skating, riding horses, diving off high dives and riding three on a bike are all activities that will likely result in kids getting injured at times, especially when these activities are performed with no or a minimum of adult supervision.

Over the years, kids in my neighborhood collectively had a few broken bones, stitches and a concussion or two. One neighborhood kid even put small objects up his nose and had to have the doctor take them out. I wonder how many pages of Big Brother regulations that that little lapse in "using the brains God gave us" spawned.

In the '50s we rode in the beds of pickup trucks, in boats being pulled on trailers and on bikes and cycles without helmets or seatbelts. The schoolyards had death traps like monkey bars and jungle gyms, and kids twelve years old carried guns while hunting in the woods. It is a miracle that there are any of our generation left.

Every year umpteen numbers of "dangerous" toys are recalled at Christmas after being identified as dangerous to kids. While we order recalls to keep our kids safe from "Mr. Mixie Dough" and his small parts, back at the ranch, this generation of young people are riding their skateboards down the rails at the local skate park, snowboarding in the back country trying to beat avalanches to the bottom of the hill and surfing waves the size of mountains. Human beings--you got to love 'em!

I am not for deliberately endangering kids but when there is a choice about permitting a risky age-appropriate activity, I am for freedom over total safety. In fact, there is no such thing as total safety. If we are to have total safety, we wouldn't get in a car or go out of our houses.

Throughout human history, kids and adults have been severely injured or killed performing certain activities. All of the laws in the world might save some, but at the cost of freedom to us all. Besides, who is to say that without so many laws, people would gain some common sense and police their own behavior?

Many "big brother knows best" laws are based on common sense and are good rules or suggestions to follow when bicycling, driving, swimming or parenting, etc. It is not necessarily wise that we make all of these good suggestions into laws. Laws take away our freedom to choose: the dangerous or the safe road, the good or bad path or the challenging or the mundane journey. They also limit our ability to make mistakes and to learn from them. Suggestions, on the other hand, are respectful of an individual's judgment and personal freedom.

One of the things that promote these invasive laws or, some would say, that gives the government an excuse to extend their authority over us, is the proliferation of liability lawsuits. Despite our twenty page disclaimers and warnings on products, we live in an era when everyone else but us are to blame for our mistakes, bad judgment and bad luck. We would have never been allowed to enter the pasture occupied by, much less sit on the backs of, a university horse today and the high dives in most public pools have long since been removed, after years of financially devastating lawsuits.

Kids today have little freedom to roam, trespass, and create their own activities or to operate without almost constant adult direction. In the performance of my job as a government employee, I have posted and/or have had fenced off many vacant public sites being used for such harmless activities as dirt bike racing, skateboarding, paint-balling, etc. The primary r reason the government and private owners post these sites is because of the danger of lawsuits.

If we had been spotted by the authorities today riding three on a bike, I'm sure we would have been stopped and cited for several infractions, including riding a bike with no shoes, riding multiple passengers, riding on the sidewalk, riding with no helmets or registration and maybe even speeding. We would have had to set up a chain of lemonade stands to pay the fines levied for those indiscretions. I don't like to think of our fate if anyone got sick on our lemonade and we weren't caring a product liability package.

If we do not want to drown in laws telling us how to do everything from feeding our kids to who we socialize with, we must take personal responsibility for the consequences of our choices. That means walking away from inappropriate lawsuits and teaching our kids to think for themselves.

I can still remember how free I felt as a kid to make my own choices, direct much of my own behavior and, if necessary, pay the price for my mistakes.

CHAPTER 9

Kids Learned Patience and Humility

My siblings and I, as did most kids in our generation, grew up learning to wait. Without microwaves or baby monitors, we waited to be picked up and to be fed. We waited our turn to be the one to get the prize out of the cereal box. We waited to get a new television until we got a new kitchen table, the house got new paint and my dad got a new lawnmower, and we waited for our shoes to wear out before we got another pair. We had to wait for others to complete having their say before we could speak. Sometimes, in the company of adults engaging in adult conversation, we had to sit quietly and say nothing and wait for our parents to decide to dismiss us. We waited for the news to be over to watch our 30 minutes of daily kid programming, and we waited to leave the dinner table until the last slow-poke, usually my sister, had finished.

Our parents never showed a morsel of regret for making us wait so much, as the belief was that waiting developed patience and humility and both were considered virtues. It is not hard to see why both patience and humility deterred a "me first" mentality.

As the third child out of four in just under five years, I certainly learned early that I wasn't the "only pebble on the beach." Pebble number one, my firstborn brother, Dwight, had an entire photo album of his first six months of life. There must be twenty pictures of him as a baby, with sunglasses on, sitting in his stroller. These pictures are all labeled with humorous handwritten captions. The days of writing captions under pictures were over in my family when pebble number two, Steve, was born. I followed along 14 months later. Baby stardom was out and sunglasses were never seen in any subsequent pictures in our now "collective" baby album.

I was the third born. Even though I came to believe the truth of the expression "the third time is the charm," that opinion was not shared by all. My arrival was so routine and uncelebrated that I was not named for several days after birth, and I never received a middle name. I suspect that my parents were too busy feeding, putting diapers on and rocking me and my two brothers to worry about digging through a baby name book.

By the time my sister Shelley arrived 18 months after me, my parents were not able to find the time to snap her first baby picture until she was about nine months old. My parents had learned that the cute little things the first baby does, like spit water out of their mouths or toss their baby food to the dog, are not as marvelous the fourth time around. Waiting for three siblings to get ready so we could leave for school, leave the dinner table or go out to play was enough. From my point of view, it was likely a good thing that my parents stopped at four.

CHAPTER 10

The Wonder of Christmas

Every kid I knew waited all year long for one day--Christmas day. It was a day that was bigger than life and it seemed to take forever to arrive. Waiting is one reason Christmas was such a Big Deal. We did not receive toys, bikes, sporting equipment or Tiny Tears dolls when we wanted them or even when we felt we needed them. If we needed a new bike or skates, we got them at Christmas or on our birthdays and not in between those two events. Christmas was really the only day of the year, except birthdays, that our parents spoiled us with material gifts of things we wanted but didn't necessarily need.

When I was about six, I began waiting in October for a zippy monkey to be found under the Christmas tree on December 25. This toy was a stuffed chimpanzee wearing a yellow shirt with his name on it, red corduroy pants with suspenders, a red hat and, best of all, some white rubber sneakers. I had an odd fascination with those sneakers because they looked and felt like marshmallows. I had never wanted anything else, other than a pony, more in my life.

After two months of waiting and nagging, I opened every present under the tree with my name on it and came up with the big ZIP... as in nothing. I was devastated and on the verge of tears. I didn't say a word. Such a display of lack of gratitude would not have gone over well. Although I thought at the time that I might be sad for months, I recovered in a day or two. Several months later, I saw a zippy monkey's head sticking out of another student's locker. The old obsession was triggered. Those marshmallow shoes were calling my name and I felt compelled to "borrow" that zippy for "show and tell." It was not a common practice to reward children back then for bad behavior. Nevertheless, the following Christmas, my grandparents took pity on me and a brand new zippy monkey with bright marshmallow shoes was waiting for me under the tree.

The zippy monkey files aside, we kids in the '50s often didn't get the thing that we most wanted, even if our parents could afford it. Our parents may have thought the item was too expensive or they may have had other priorities. In either case, we likely did not get an explanation of WHY we hadn't received the desired thing. We were sad but not angry because we didn't feel entitled to get whatever we asked for and, besides, possessions had not yet become the objects of worship, prestige and even obsession that they so often are today. Kids today have even killed their parents when they did not get the presents they desired.

We learned from an early age that "getting" wasn't a matter of life and death and that we really didn't need everything we thought we needed to be happy. Therefore, we were not as obsessed with material goods as kids are today. In fact, it was considered immature and un-cool to go around flaunting one's stuff or trying to "top" one's neighbor in terms of new acquisitions.

It was around Christmas time that I first heard the phrase "keeping up with the Joneses." In whatever lecture that my parents brought the "Jones" family up, they always made it clear that it was disgraceful to compete with that family because of social pressure. For a short period of time when I was about five, I wondered who the "Joneses" were. I didn't like the idea that this family, whom I had never met, was in some sort of competition with my family. My dad didn't seem very interested in the competition but I made up my mind that if I ever encountered these people, I would show them that our family could not only "keep up" with but could surpass their family any day of the week.

Many years later I remember the fleeting look of puzzlement on my son's face when I asked him why he believed that he was leading the "life of Riley." Just as I was preparing to answer his questions about who this "Riley" person was, he changed the topic. Unlike me, my son rarely ruminated about stuff as a kid and he never listens very closely to what I say. So, he accepted the comment and never questioned me about this guy Riley and why he (Erik) would be living someone else's life.

Like today, Christmas in the 1950s included giving and getting presents. We also baked candy and pastries and decorated the house. In addition, Christmas back then was more than the activities that it involved. It was a time, an atmosphere, a collective feeling of goodwill and hope. The story of Jesus' birth and destiny were on people's minds. We kids were taught every year in school, home and church why we celebrated Christmas. We performed in Christmas plays at school and listened to the teacher in Sunday school.

Even when we were just little kids, we wished people a "Merry Christmas" and we talked and sang about the first Christmas. Christmas carols were played on every radio station. Every Christmas Eve, we attended candlelight services at our church and heard again the wonder of the Christmas story and sang about *Emmanuel* (God with us).

As we outgrew the "Santa Claus" years, Christmas became less and less about getting stuff and more and more about the good news, the love of God and goodwill toward mankind. The ageless carols and the beauty and mystery of the Christmas story were already such a part of our memories and celebration of Christmas that they quickly supplanted our fascination with Santa.

The following verses of some of the most well-known Christmas carols are so obviously inspired by the love of God that I suspect that these carols alone have led some to respond to the calling of their Lord to return to Him.

Silent Night, Holy night
Son of God, love's pure light

Radiant beams from Thy holy face
With the dawn of redeeming Grace...
Silent Night, Gruber and Mohr

Still through the cloven skies they come,
With peaceful wings unfurled;
And still their heavenly music floats
O'er all the weary world.
It Came Upon the Midnight Clear, Edmund Sears

Most children of the '50s are also very familiar with the "Christmas" Bible scriptures. Even as a child, I felt overwhelmed with the mystery and hope contained in the following scripture:

Fear not: for, behold, I bring you good tidings of great joy, which shall be to all people. For unto you is born this day in the city of David a Savior, which is Christ the Lord. And this shall be a sign unto you: Ye shall find the babe wrapped in swaddling clothes, lying in a manger. And suddenly there was with the angel a multitude of the heavenly host praising God, and saying, Glory to God in the highest, and on earth peace, good will toward men. Luke 2:13-14

An individual's behavior during the Christmas season reflected the spiritual principles upon which the celebration of Christmas rested. People were kinder and friendlier as they embraced the spirit of Christmas in their hearts. Our increased kindness toward others often resulted in "charity" work, such as taking presents to the elderly or shut-ins. What we did for one another back then was freely given, not some government-mandated program or for-show volunteer work.

Christmas was a time when people went out of their way to perform acts of kindness. Sometimes our school classroom would go on a field trip to visit those who were alone or disabled and shut in for the holidays. We brought food, small gifts and a smile. In particular, I remember the return smiles on those sick elderly faces in nursing homes or the scared faces of the little kids in the hospitals. We were learning little by little the truth of the saying *it is more blessed to give than receive.*

One of the ways our neighbors gave to each other at Christmas time was to drop by with homemade candy or pastries. A few days before Christmas, neighbors would come to our house caroling. I can still picture them standing in the snow in our front yard, holding candles, and singing those old traditional songs. We would invite them in to warm up with hot cider or cocoa and offer them cookies and cakes.

I recall the feelings of safety and fullness that I felt just sitting and chatting with our neighbors in the warmth of our kitchen, while the cold wind blew and drifted the snow outside. Sometimes the carolers would shovel our walk or porch when they left, and sometimes we would put on our boots, mittens, hats and coats and go with them to carol at the next house.

The Bible says that Jesus was born into our world for a reason. "Greater Love hath no man than this… that a man lay down his life for his friend." That is the bar that Jesus set. No human will ever do for mankind what Jesus did because none of us are perfect, but as we try to show our love for others, we will be transformed from the inside out.

Times have changed, however. No longer can one count on hearing the Christmas carols in the malls and no longer do we hear the Bible scriptures on public radio. Our society has journeyed away from God and the Golden Rule and toward a worship of mankind and selfish gain. The "me first" mentality is now dominant and the accompanying alienation, depression and anger are now frequently the "new" face of our society year-round, as well as during that formerly most wonderful season.

CHAPTER 11

Families Played and Stayed Together

One of the most ridiculous ideas that came into vogue in the past half century is that we must "love and take care of ourselves before we can love or take care of others." It is of course a partner to the "me first" world view. The implication is that this self-love will not only make us happy but it will equip us to be good to others. Looking at this from the other direction, we have been told that if we don't take care of ourselves first, we will have nothing to give to others. No matter how many "experts" endorse this, I have never seen it work.

On my street there were perhaps twenty-four families. There was not one divorce in the twenty years I lived on that street, and I have not heard of one since I left thirty-five year ago. People stuck it out through the good and bad. They made it through the tough times and they and their children benefited. Second marriages are more likely to end than first ones and there is something to be said for growing old with your kids other parent and the companion of your youth. The truth is the idea that we should "take care of one's own needs first" would have been considered hedonistic in the 50s.

One way today's adults attempt to," take care of themselves," is to go on getaway vacations from the family or kids. Most families vacationed together when I was a kid and the expression "adult vacations" was unknown. My parents never took a vacation by themselves until my siblings and I were older. They may have gone on a business trip for a few days, but that was it until I was in high school. In the '50s families vacationed together even if it meant parents did not get to "take care of themselves first."

Looking back, I realize how much family vacations bonded us together. We were bonded by the time and the experiences we had and then, over the years, by the memories. I believe that my parents enjoyed the making of those collective family memories as much as we did. I am thankful that their generation didn't believe they needed to find themselves or be good to themselves at the expense of their children's emotionally healthy childhoods.

Prices were running about 18.9 to 25.0 cents a gallon for gas in the '50s so very few people flew and road trips were in. My dad was forced to take all of his vacation time at once so every summer we took up to a three or four week road trip in our station wagon. During my childhood we traveled thorough every state in the continental United States except Oregon. We saw most of the national parks and monuments. We went to the Seattle World's fair via the Badlands, the Black Hills, the Bighorn Mountains and Yellowstone and the Grand Tetons National Park. We looked in awe at the views from Trail Ridge in the Rocky Mountains and the Going to The Sun Highway in Glacier. The years we went to Florida and New England, we drove the beautiful Blue Ridge parkway that stretches between the Great Smoky Mountains and the Shenandoah National Parks.

We pulled our motor boat so we could use it but, more importantly, so we could fill it with camping equipment. Pull campers were few and most everyone tented back then, and this made camping a lot more social than it is today. The interstates weren't completed yet so roads were mostly two lanes and they led into and down the main street of every little town on the route. I remember how my dad had to pull our car and boat over to the side of the road every 20-30 miles to let frustrated traffic pass.

These trips were sometimes a time of testing for our family, with two adults and four kids stuffed in a station wagon together all day long.

Hours of travel with the hot wind and smell of exhaust coming in through the back window proved challenging, especially in the humid Southeastern and Western desert states. Our car did not have an air conditioner, and it had only four window seats. Those with the weakest stomachs sat next to the windows.

Yours truly and my youngest brother, who spent half the day reading in the car, had the cast iron stomachs. My younger sister, on the other hand, frequently required the window seat. Her genuine need was proven on one or two occasions when we were all treated to a revisitation of her last meal. Despite this, my brother the reader and I suspected that at times she feigned illness in order to avail herself of the window seat. Her smug look as she basked in the cool wind (relative to the stagnant air in the car) coming in the open window didn't help to dispel my younger brother's and my suspicions. At night we would set up two tents. My parents needed the privacy to face the next day. We kids found that the privacy of our tent, away from our parents' watchful eyes and ears, was a good place to settle grievances from earlier that day.

I remember looking out the car window and seeing countless other station wagons with car top carriers and out of state license plates stuffed full with kids and their moms and dads. Sometimes chaos reined in those cars and parents could be seen swatting at the kids in the back seats with maps or, as was the case with my dad, other more deadly objects, such as yardsticks. At more peaceful times, one could see the kids eating ice cream cones while the parents calmly pointed out objects of historical interest. We were the '50s middle class version of Woody Guthrie or John Steinbeck discovering America.

For all of the magnificent sites we saw, what has stuck in my mind over these past fifty years are the people we met. We met them in the gas stations, restaurants, camp grounds and motels. We met them in the stores and the roadside produce stands. We met them on tours of the national parks and the national wonders. We met them at clam bakes in Maine and white fish fries in Door County, Wisconsin. We met them while we sat anchored in our boat on Lake Coeur de Lane, Idaho, watching the precision F-16 squadron, the Thunderbirds, perform.

Everywhere we went, from Florida to Maine to the West Coast, the people of our great country greeted us. They were open, honest, helpful and friendly. I learned from an early age that there were good people wherever one went. In all of our travels we never had a theft. a fight or even harsh words, with other travelers. Everywhere we went felt like home. This was the beginning of my affection for and optimism about the American people.

Although road trips took longer back then, they seemed more personal and I felt more connected to our country than I do today riding thousands of miles on interstates. On rare occasions, there was silence in our car. I recall riding in the back seat with my head resting part-way out the window, caught up in my own thoughts. I would sing quietly to myself knowing that the sound of my off-key renditions of my favorite songs would be blotted out by the wind noise that was almost deafening when all four windows were open. At those times, with my father driving, surrounded by my family, I felt safer than any other time in my life that I can remember.

Whether it was day or night, sun or rain, we were together in our little fortress of a car, going down the roads in a free country filled with trustworthy people to places we had never seen before. I recall thinking that someday I would grow up and move away to live on my own and raise my own children. It never crossed my mind that when that day came, divorce and a general decaying value system would fracture my own family and deprive my son and much of his generation of the sense of safety and optimism for the future that much of my generation took for granted.

In the summer, when we weren't off vacationing, we spent many weekends at the local lakes as a family with other families, boating and waterskiing. When the winter came, our family traveled almost every weekend together to the adjoining states--Michigan, Wisconsin, Minnesota, and Ohio--for speed skating meets. We kids raced from dawn until sometimes 10 pm almost every winter Friday night and Saturday and Sunday during the day. This involved my parents driving anywhere from 250 to 900 miles a weekend and spending scarce money on restaurants and motels.

I think of the work and stress of taking four kids on a 5000 plus mile vacation trip or on a 550 mile trip to a skating meet. Putting the tents up and down, putting the boat on and off the water, cooking on camp stoves and then driving all day was no one's idea of "taking care of oneself first." In the winter, preparing for races and driving all day long in winter conditions was grueling. Was this really how my parents wanted to spend their time off? When I look back I see that my parents did not "take care of themselves first." They were too busy taking care of the family.

"To every thing there is a season," the Bible says. My parents and their generation lived according to the seasons of one's life. They didn't try to remain children once they became adults, as many of my generation have, and they didn't attempt to live like a retired couple whose children were grown and gone while we kids were young.

During the years of our family vacations, I never heard my dad or mom say anything about being deprived of a relaxing adult only trip to the Bahamas or some such place. I'm sure that, when the time came and we kids were grown, my mom and dad enjoyed those well-earned adult-only vacations. I believe they were much more enjoyable because my parents knew that they had spent years sacrificing in their roles as responsible parents. It's possible that in caring for others they met their own needs and that happiness is more a result of doing for others than for oneself.

My parents didn't tell my siblings and me that they loved us very often, but they showed us how much they valued us by the sacrifices they willingly made every day.

CHAPTER 12

Friendship, Kindness, Generosity

In the 1950s, faith, standards, and traditions encouraged and sustained far more emotionally stable and harmonious relationships than we have today. People actually did things for each other without having an agenda beyond being a good neighbor and investing in relationships that they knew would likely last for decades. The Golden Rule was manifested through the virtues of kindness, generosity, fairness, understanding and forgiveness in neighborhoods throughout the country.

People had "friends" during my childhood. Sometime in the last 50 years, many of us began developing contacts and building networks. Lasting friendship requires loyalty, understanding, honesty and sacrifice. Networks or spheres of influence involve favors, sacrifices and compromise but with strings attached. In networks, these favors are often like a deposit in a bank. Favors are performed and deposited with the expectation of future withdrawals.

When I was growing up, neighbors were always doing things for each other. There was a relaxed give–and–take approach to favors that I rarely see today. Of course, people understood that good relationships made it easier to request favors; however, it was the desire for friendship and the goodwill of one's neighbors that motivated people to freely give to each other, not the expectations of reciprocal favors down the road.

In fact, our neighbors very rarely requested favors of other neighbors. Instead, neighbors in the '50s often did small favors for each other, such as baking an extra pan of fresh sweet rolls for a neighbor whose child was ill or picking up an extra staple on sale at the grocery store for a friend. In my neighborhood, a neighbor who was an electrician would troubleshoot others' electrical problems and the local vet would check out dog and cat complaints, as well as neighborhood children on several occasions. My dad was an entomologist and was the neighborhood consultant on garden pests. It was like a neighborhood co-op but without the formality.

The social taboo against "using people" was so strong that neighborliness rarely deteriorated into the parasitical relationships that we see today. In fact, there was a strict unspoken code of conduct that dictated how people treated each other and each other's property.

For instance, adults did not borrow money from each other. Sometimes, however, a kid would borrow money from another kid. If the parents knew of the debt they would see to it that every penny was returned. We kids were taught at a young age that it was not about the amount of money; it was about "the principle of the thing." So all debts were treated pretty much the same, whether they were for $4.00 or $40.00.

The Golden Rule dictated that we have respect for other people's property. If a kid left something at another kid's house, that item was set aside and returned to the owner as soon as possible. These days there is a different game: the one that says if no one asks for it, the one in possession gets to keep it.

Even when my mom borrowed a cup of sugar or an egg, it was always returned. Borrowing was borrowing and not taking. If we did borrow anything from a friend and that property was damaged while in our custody, it was almost always fixed or replaced by the borrower. Even if the borrower wasn't responsible for the damage, if the item was in the borrower's custody when it broke, the borrower assumed responsibility and went out of their way to make things right and fair. The key was that people were trying to do what was fair, not what would be best for them personally.

During my childhood, all of the parents shared the responsibility for feeding, watching and transporting the neighborhood kids. We kids often ate at the house we were playing in when lunchtime came. I remember at one house, lunch was often Kool-Aid and bologna, Jell-O, peanut butter and jelly sandwiches or macaroni and cheese. In the morning, the mom of that house served a new thing called *frozen waffles*. It was always a lucky day when we ended up at that house at mealtime, although I expect that today the food police would have something to say and a few laws to write about the menu.

The using behavior that is so common today would have been considered very odd and deviant when I was young. Unlike today, perpetrators 50 years ago would have paid a high social price for damaging and not repairing another's property, not repaying a debt or constantly accepting favors without returning any. Although it was unspoken, the code was so consistently obeyed that people were more relaxed about asking for and accepting favors, because they knew that things wouldn't get out of hand.

One snowy winter day, my family had some fun with our neighbor who, over the twenty years our families lived next door to each other, did many favors for us, as we did for him. When my father was out of town on business and my brothers were still little and it would snow, this neighbor would stop by and shovel our driveway and sidewalk out. I suppose this would be considered chauvinistic today, but my mother greatly appreciated it.

Once, during a heavy snowstorm, my dad got home early and put the car in the garage. Our neighbor, thinking my dad was out of town, came over and began shoveling. My dad, who had been getting into his boots to go outside, decided to play a trick on our kind-hearted neighbor. We all sat and laughed as we watched from behind the drapes as our neighbor laboriously shoveled the snow off our driveway.

Just as he was finishing up the driveway, my dad went outside and thanked him for the excellent job he had done. He chased my dad with the shovel, but after an hour of shoveling, our poor misused neighbor didn't have a chance of catching my freshly rested-up dad. Later we had our still-friendly neighbor and his family over for dessert and coffee.

On another occasion, my mom presented this same kind-hearted neighbor with a jar of homemade jam that looked yummy but turned out to be harder than a brick. When the unlucky recipient discovered this as he was having his toast the next morning, he plotted his revenge. Waiting patiently until Christmas, he wrapped up the jam and gave it back to our family in an unmarked package under the tree. We passed that brick of jam back and forth many times over the years, and we became more and more adept and creative at disguising and hiding it as time went by. It was our little personal joke, and the laughter and friendship we felt grew as the years went by.

Looking back, I realize how lucky we kids were to have grown up in a place and time when not only was our nuclear family intact but we had a backup support system in neighbors who were truly friends in many of the ways that best define that word. It was the belief in "doing unto others as we would have them do unto us" that grew the friendships, and it was the friendships that surrounded us like a warm security blanket.

CHAPTER 13

Open Spaces and Open Lives

The houses on my street were small but they were all different and because they were new, the landscaping was very simple. There were not many hedges and in the early years, there weren't any fences. It was considered somewhat un-neighborly to put up a fence, and the few neighbors who eventually put up fences would go out of their way to assure their adjoining property owners that it wasn't "personal."

The lack of fences forced neighbors to get to know each other. Neighbors met and talked while mowing their lawns, burning their leaves, hanging out the laundry, painting the house or playing catch with their kids. Neighbors spoke to each other in driveways, while getting the mail, taking out garbage and getting the milk that was delivered to the milkboxes. Houses were homes, not investments, and most people lived in the same homes for many decades, so it made good sense to develop pleasant relationships with those who lived nearby. Many neighbors, like my parents, played bridge with each other, participated in activities together and celebrated holidays together.

As for us kids, we never knew anything but wide open spaces. We played our football, baseball, tag and winter snow fort games in three or four adjacent wide open yards. At night we played hide and seek in five or six yards on both sides of the street. The neighbors never complained that we were trespassing.

Even the dogs ran free. Although this was sometimes dangerous to both dogs and humans, the dogs loved it. People watched their dogs and when they saw them answer nature's big call on another neighbor's yard, they would go and retrieve it. The key word in that sentence is "when" and so we kids had to watch where we stepped.

I realize this may seem gross to some of you, but think about what the situation was just sixty years earlier. The antelope, deer, bears and miscellaneous wildlife all wandered and "answered the call of nature" where they pleased. In the '50s, occasionally cleaning off one's sneakers and the breaking up of an occasional dogfight with a hose was the price we paid for the freedom the dogs and cats had.

My brother, Steve, and I spent many summer days and nights chasing butterflies with nets and lightning bugs with jars in and across yards all over the neighborhood. As long as we didn't trample the flowers or vegetable gardens, we were almost always permitted in any yard on the block. Sometimes owners would even come out to see what kind of butterfly we were chasing or help us catch it.

In the spring, we would fly kites out of sight, which always meant "until the string broke", and then we would undertake the inevitable chase across umpteen neighbors' yards to retrieve what was left of it. The only time I recall being blocked from our pursuits was when we tried to climb up a neighbor's trellis to get on their roof, where our kite was ensnared in their television antenna. My brother was on the roof and I was worming my way up the trellis when we heard a voice say something like "What is going on here? You kids get down this minute or I am calling your folks." We were down on the ground in a nanosecond. The neighbor explained that we would have to let the kite go because the roof was too dangerous for kids. In those days, when there were almost no lawsuits, we knew that our neighbor was genuinely concerned about our welfare rather than his liability.

Today fences are everywhere and they serve two primary purposes, privacy and protection. In my town in the '50s, people were not as obsessed with privacy as they are today, and protection was not an issue.

The need for increased protection/security today is no mystery but our growing obsession with privacy is not so easily explained. Many live in communities where every house has a six-foot fence and where people enter and exit through an automatic garage door. These days, our contact with the outside world is more often a cell phone (or Facebook) rather than a face–to-face encounter. Why does it seem that we are more and more determined to keep our neighbors at a distance?

Maybe part of the answer is we don't want to be bothered with getting to know our neighbors because they might need something from us, like our time, concern or (gulp) even our "stuff." Further, as we become more selfish in our deeds and thoughts and subsequently more alienated from our fellow man, we understandably want more "privacy." The Bible talks about man's desire to hide his bad behavior by hiding in the darkness.

"And this is the condemnation, that Light is come into the world, and men loved darkness rather than light, because their deeds were evil. John 3:19, NIV.

The more we isolate ourselves, the darker our lives seem. This increasing physical isolation has gone hand-in-hand with increasing loneliness and alienation. It's hard to like or even understand people that you don't know. The other day I heard on the news that one in five Americans is mentally ill and can be assigned a psychiatric diagnosis. The highest incidence was in the 18-25 year old group. This is no surprise, as the types of relationships that make for good mental health are based on the Golden Rule, not the "me-first" mentality.

About a year ago a man in my town took a shotgun on Easter and went to his neighbor of twenty-five years' house and killed the man and woman living there. The story goes that the killer was angry because for years the victims and their friends had parked in front of his place and done "turnarounds" in the killer's driveway. WHAT? So the only alternative was to shoot one's neighbors down?

I do not recall any incidents such as this one when I was growing up. First, the parties involved would likely have talked it out before it reached the point of violence. Other neighbors would have acted as intermediaries and encouraged the peace. Second, the arrogance that allows a person to take another's life because they are irritated was almost non-existent in the '50s. Lastly, the isolation and detachment that neighbors said the killer displayed was also extremely rare when I was growing up.

CHAPTER 14

Remorse, Confession, and Forgiveness Kept Peace in the "Hood."

Everything was not always peaceful among neighbors in the '50s. In our travels across other people's property, sometimes we kids got careless and ran into the flower beds or vegetable gardens. A stern "You kids get out of there" yelled from the porch or a phone call to our parents was enough to get us in line. In those days, when other adults called our parents to report misbehavior, the caller could almost always count on our parents' full support.

I recall one night my friends and I were playing a game of tag called "The Ghost Comes Out Tonight", and I got the bright idea to hide on top of a neighbor's grapevine trestle. It turned out to be the perfect choice. I was able to observe the activities of the other players from a high place without being caught. It was such a good spot that my friends gave up looking for me and went in their houses, leaving me cleverly hiding for another half hour, until I finally realized the game was over. When I went in the house, my parents pointed out the grape stains on my clothes, and so the next day, I was sent to the neighbors to apologize for lying on top of their grapes.

My parents didn't wait for a call from the wronged party or hope the grapes' owners hadn't noticed their squished grapes. My parents' goal was to teach me to respect other people's property and to admit to my mistakes, not to maintain the appearance that they had raised a well-behaved child which, in my case, would have been a Herculean task.

Over the years my siblings and I found ourselves apologizing to our neighbors fairly regularly. My personal rap sheet included shooting arrows straight up and out of sight into the blue sky, until one "came to earth" very close to a neighbor hanging out her laundry three houses down. I was out looking for my lost arrow when I saw our irate neighbor stomping down the street, arrow in hand. I chose to take a little trip on my bike and let the situation cool down. When I returned, I was forced to make the usual "mea culpa" visit to the wronged party, who must have asked me, "What were you thinking?" or "Are you mentally retarded?" at least five times.

On another occasion when I had a "mental lapse," I cut a batch of our neighbor's prize roses and went door to door selling them. A shrill scream from the victim's backyard told me my unsolicited pruning had been discovered. As I recall, the grower was able to locate me in a matter of minutes, as each successive neighbor whose house I had visited in the hopes of selling those fine roses pointed their fingers in the direction they had last seen me meandering.

There was such a ruckus over this misdemeanor that my mom heard it and was drawn to investigate. With four kids, my mom had learned that there was always a good chance one of us was in the center of any disturbance, as was the case this time. I was immediately divested of my meager profits, which were given to the once-proud owner of the best rose garden in the neighborhood and the mother of my best friend. I apologized on the spot and again every time I saw this neighbor for the next several months and over time, our neighbor seemed to forget the ugly incident.

I do recall several other incidents of "bad judgment" on my or my siblings' part which required a reconciliation visit to some neighbor's house. The transgressions included participating in a tree-house building project whose source of lumber was a nearby home construction site, disabling a neighbor's laundry rack by swinging on it, getting stuck inside a neighbor's doghouse, accidentally shooting out a window with a BB gun, peeking at a friend's father's "Playboy" magazine and participating in the building of a bike jumping ramp in the middle of the street.

The all-time favorite activity in the neighborhood when we were bored was ringing doorbells and running away before the occupant came to the door. Sometimes we would return to the same door twice and even three times in the same night. There was no thrill like it, because by the third time it was for sure that the neighbor would have made preparations to catch us.

I know some readers are right now counting their blessings that they never had my family as neighbors, and I have to admit that some kids caught on to the wisdom of the Golden Rule faster than others.

Our neighbors always accepted our apologies and no one held grudges, at least not openly. Friction between neighbors with kids and the few without was greatly reduced because of the cooperation of the kid's parents and the contrition of the kid. Neighbors could be sure that the offending kid "got what he/she deserved from their parents," including a spanking if necessary and this administering of justice went a long way in helping the victims forgive the crimes.

We kids were always respectful to adults and to the day they died, I referred to the adults I knew as a child as Mr. and Mrs. Whoever rather than disrespect them by using their first names. In retrospect, it wasn't that we kids were perfect fifty years ago. But when we did act wrongly and inconsiderately, we and our parents acknowledged that we were wrong and tried to make it right. These days, parents frequently get so defensive about complaints regarding their kids that other adults are often reluctant to report a kid's bad behavior, fearing retribution from the parents or the kids.

On the other hand, there seems to be less and less tolerance for the bad judgment of youth. Too many adults today have forgotten the excesses and mistakes of their own youth. It's as though our society has gone from seeing youthful misbehaving as Huck Finn misadventures to branding all misbehaving youth as potential Columbine shooters.

Remorse and forgiveness are two vanishing manifestations of the Golden Rule. Unfortunately, in our "me first" society there is little advantage to confessing or apologizing, and forgiving is far less popular than *getting even*.

As we bring our visit to the '50s to a close I want to reaffirm a reality about that place in time that we should not forget. It was not perfect. People were not perfect. In general, people back then believed in and lived by the Ten Commandments and the Golden Rule and to the extent that they did, the quality of everyone's lives was improved.

Christmas Time - Dwight, Me, Shelley, Steve with giant candy-canes.

Easter Sunday- Feel the love! Me, Steve, Shelley, Dwight

The Moore Family Skaters-Steve, Shelley, me, Dwight in back.

Heading out on vacation- Me looking out back window.

My parents visiting California

Lonnie, Me, Scott- Awaiting the plastic surgeon.

Erik –The joy of my life

Wabana Lake-Taken off my parent's porch- Where I was saved.

PART III

Things Changed

CHAPTER 16

The World Turned Upside Down

When we talk about the '60s we are generalizing about a time period that falls between perhaps 1965 and around 1972. Most historians agree that the 1960s was a time of dramatic change for our society. Of course this change didn't suddenly start in the '60s. Like a wave that originates across the ocean and is seen only when it crashes on shore, the origins of the '60s had their beginnings long ago. There are some events that impacted and accelerated the rate of change however. Some pinpoint the disillusionment following President John Kennedy's assassination in 1963 as the critical turning point where our nation began traveling away from innocence and optimism towards the darker side of human nature.

I was twelve at the time of President Kennedy's assassination, and it certainly shook my formerly stable world. In my short life, I had never seen such vulnerability and chaos in our country as was exposed by that one act. For the first time, I could see that adults were not all-powerful or all-knowing. When I think of how young kids are today when they learn that lesson, it makes me sad for their lost childhoods.

One of our nation greatest conflicts, racism, grew out of our nations greatest injustice, slavery. Ninety years after the Civil War, blacks were still being denied some of our nation's basic freedoms. Beginning in the late '50s, the civil rights movement was gathering steam in an attempt to level the playing field for access to voting, jobs, schools, promotions, etc. Many of the civil rights songs spoke of God, justice, and brotherly love. The civil rights movement was all about doing unto others as we would have them do unto us, and so it was consistent with the Golden Rule that we baby boomers had been brought up with.

The non-violent tactics and strategies of the civil rights movement, which were role modeled by Gandhi and adopted by Martin Luther King, were also consistent with the values that the baby boomers were raised with. Although winning was extremely important for the future of every black American, King believed that it was important to adhere to the "it's how you play the game" philosophy in order to maintain the moral authority to ask for support for civil rights for blacks. King also was a true believer in Jesus Christ, and he held on tight to his Christian beliefs in the midst of hatred, violence and gross injustices.

In the face of extreme violence from the opposition, MLK refused to abandon his commitment to non-violence and the Golden Rule. Most of the baby boomers, including myself, very much admired the courage and dedication of Rev. King. We also noted that, although Dr. King followed the rules, he was treated like a criminal and ultimately he was murdered.

In the mid- to late '60s, an entirely new youth culture appeared. There were distinctive cultural, political and social attributes to this new youth culture. The baby boomers began wearing long hair, tie-dyed shirts with bell bottomed jeans and listening to rebellious music. Someone labeled us hippies after the word "hip", a common slang word coined by the prior "beat" generation. Aside from our distinctive clothes and the guys' long hair, many boomer hippies smoked pot and did hallucinogenic drugs such as mescaline, peyote and LSD. We also became more and more anti-American and anti-capitalistic as time went on.

So after grabbing some riot gear and a bail bond number, let's get back in the DeLorean and head to the 1960s.

CHAPTER 17

No Going Back

I graduated from high school in 1969, the year of Woodstock. I was all set to go to that now infamous cultural "coming out party" for the boomers, but I broke my ankle a week before high school graduation. After consuming at least six beers I had jumped off the back steps of a youth house called the "Other Side." This little taxpayer supported social experiment named after The Door's lyrics "break on through to the other side," was a good example of the emerging new liberal thinking on how to solve social problems with tax-supported programs and freebies.

The "Other Side" was a large multi-storied house on the university campus which the city rented to provide a place for the high school youth of the town to meet and socialize away from the prying eyes of adults. Although we were never quite sure WHY the city taxpayers were funding this joint, we young people were nevertheless glad to have a place that provided us with the privacy, safety and companionship that we needed to enjoy the sex, drugs and rock and roll that we felt entitled to.

I was a frequent visitor to the "Other Side" and was quite familiar with the activities on site. Generally there would be approximately 15-20 high school students scattered throughout the ten-plus rooms in the house. Some students would be engaging in various levels of sex in the walk-in closets, while others would be partaking of drugs or alcohol.

During a weekday, most everyone at the "Other Side" was skipping school. I was there a lot during school hours and although I didn't spend much time in the closets, I was very willing to partake of the drugs and alcohol available. I can barely remember my senior year of high school. I do know that I graduated with fifty-plus active detentions and a significant drug habit that included LSD.

Not long after the "Other Side" opened, the local newspaper did a whitewashed story on the goings-on at that establishment. This article gave the illusion that this place was an educational facility for young people. I do recall one "theater of the absurd" play by Samuel Beckett being presented in the house. It was *Waiting for Godot*, a play in which the main character waits endlessly for "God" to show up. I guess one could also call what went on in the closet an *education*. I recall that several of us regulars had a good laugh when we read that article that was so far from the truth.

The neighbors, who had a birds-eye view of the "goings-on," had a little different opinion of what they called "the devil's playhouse." However, their first hand observations were dismissed as a NIMBY (not in my backyard) reaction and the "Other Side" remained open.

Much to my dismay, Woodstock was not postponed due to my disabled condition and my disloyal friends went without me. I never heard the end of it. After having missed that historic event, I was determined not to spend another second on the sidelines of what was shaping up as a very exciting era.

Thereafter, I sampled as many areas of the '60s cultural and political lifestyle as time allowed. I engaged in coast-to-coast hitchhiking, lived in a hippie commune and showed up for youth international party be-ins. I joined an SDS cadre, went to Washington, D.C., twice and went to jail three times in two years. I hitchhiked to San Francisco with fifty dollars and managed to stay the whole summer there and in Boulder, Colorado, by panhandling and selling blood when the fifty ran out. I managed to see, among many others, Van Morrison, Jethro Tull, Jimmy

Hendricks, Jefferson Airplane, Janice Joplin and the Rolling Stones in concert and to see "Fantasia" on acid.

Many things changed for me as well as our nation between 1967 (the year I started drugs and officially became a hippie) and when I graduated from college in 1973. I entered college in 1969, the year the political rebellion in our country reached explosive levels.

CHAPTER 18

Vietnam and Revolution 101

After the civil rights legislation was passed, the Vietnam War became the unifying issue for the baby boomers as well as the lightning rod for our growing anger and disillusionment. Like the civil rights movement, the anti-war movement was originally about concern for others. We wanted to save the lives of both our own soldiers and the soldiers and civilians of North and South Vietnam.

As previously noted, the baby boomers had a clear sense of right and wrong behavior and we initially did not promote behavior that harmed others or violated their civil rights, even if it promoted our cause. In the early years of the anti-war movement we followed the standards that we had learned growing up and which had been exemplified by Martin Luther King's life. We held peaceful demonstrations and practiced peaceful resistance tactics.

I will always remember my first Washington, D.C., demonstration. It was the Moratorium in November 1969. It was the largest anti-war demonstration ever held in our nation's capitol. Attendees came from almost every university and state. There were between 400,000 and 800,000 people in attendance. Other than a small ruckus at the Pentagon, it was dignified and peaceful. Whether one agreed with the cause or not, this demonstration showcased the best of the '60s... peaceful, respectful, democratic and full of "good vibes."

I rode one of eight buses from my university a thousand miles to our nation's capital. I had never seen that many people gathered together before. As I met people from all over the country, our common cause, our student status and our similar ages made us instant friends. People were giving away their food, offering shelter and raising bail money for the few who had been arrested. We were looking after each other in the best spirit of the Golden Rule and of the early years of the hippie movement.

We listened to the music of Peter, Paul and Mary, the Mamas and the Papas, Buddy Miles, and Crosby, Stills and Nash. Most of the songs and speeches bore a socio-political message but the extreme anger and vilification of our opponents was not yet evident.

A combination of my age (18), being in Washington, D.C., the famous bands and speakers and the masses of people gave the whole event a surrealistic aura. To me it seemed almost mystical as the sea of humanity between the Washington monument and the Lincoln Memorial moved and swayed as though it were a single being. It was like a scene out of some epic movie as the hundreds of thousands of mostly young people ate, talked and mingled together in the green areas that surround our most famous national monuments.

There were no strangers, no beautiful or ugly, no disabled, no "in crowds" or cliques and no divisive racism. I felt a sense of power, pride and hope as well as a feeling of belonging to and being at peace with the whole human race, or at least 400,000-800,000 of them.

I was young, naïve, arrogant and stoned enough to believe that we, the youth of America, were charting a new course in human history by putting people ahead of things and tearing down the superficial divisions that separated us. Looking back, I truly believe that this sense of being "one as a generation" and the deep desire of every human being to connect with others was the engine that drove the '60s as much as or more than the Vietnam War did.

This massive get-together was a political coming of age statement by the baby boomers, as Woodstock had been a cultural statement. We, the new generation, were showing that we would not be bound by the "old rules" of social interaction. Our doors would be open to people of all races, economic and educational backgrounds. Further, we were comfortable with group living and group identity. We were a large generation and we would use our numbers collectively to produce change. We would support each other emotionally and economically. We believed that materialism had gone too far and that it was time to put people ahead of things.

Harmony, peace, brotherly and sisterly love were what we hoped for. Were these idealistic and naïve concepts? Yes. Were these ideals wrong to seek and strive for? No. So what happened? Why couldn't we "just get along?" The attributes which corrupted our good intentions grew out of selfishness. Pride, anger, jealousy and the desire for power and recognition defeated our good intentions in the '60s. These same common weaknesses of mankind have prevented peace and freedom for much of the human population since the beginning of time.

So, we took our idealism and went out into the real world to live by our ideals. Later that year, I actually moved into a commune. I anticipated working together and helping each other on a voluntary basis with housework, cooking and errands etc. I quickly discovered why Marx said we had to have a dictatorship of the proletariat. Human nature does not of its own free will sacrifice indefinitely for others without some return. Since many of us naively believed that people would naturally do the fair thing if given the chance, we initially dispensed with rules or even guidelines for behavior. There was no positive or negative reinforcement. Hence, ill manners ruled and violations of other people's space, personal property and quiet time were routine. Cleaning, doing the dishes and even just picking up the place quickly fell to the standards of the messiest person in the house. Some people went to paper plates and cups and others ate and quietly placed their dirty dishes on the stack for that day that never came, when someone else would do them. Our kitchen began to look like something on the front of a Rolling Stones Album.

As for paying one's way and buying food, cleaning products, etc., once again, only a few of the occupants felt obliged to participate. The majority dug through the available food and picked out whatever appealed to them and ate it, whether they had bought it or not. At the end of the year when students moved out for the summer, those foolish enough to have signed the rental contracts were often stuck with large unpaid collective phone and utility bills. Needless to say, I was looking for other "digs" within the year.

Many of us were disappointed that reality and ideals were so far apart and that harmony and fairness among people was not the norm. We were also fining a large gap between our idealism and reality in the political arena. The anti-war movement was meeting stronger and sometimes violent resistance from the "establishment." As the government and universities responded, sometimes with violence, to our increasingly violent demonstrations, the radical element of the movement grew in numbers and our tactics became more and more aggressive.

CHAPTER 19

Pre-emptive Reciprocity

By the beginning of 1970, the radical faction of the antiwar movement was dominating. Our role models and mentors were no longer Gandhi or Martin Luther King. We had seen what happened to people like King and Robert Kennedy, who followed the rules. We increasingly embraced the teachings of radicals like Regis Debray, Mao Zedong, Ho Chi Minh, Eldridge Cleaver, Che Guevara, Frantz Fanon, and Mark Rudd.

Most of the radical leaders were Marxists or Socialists. Sometime during the '60s the movement became more about "revolution" than about anything else including the war.

As time passed, the more radical cultural element, the Youth International Party, or Yippies, and the more leftist politicos, i.e., the Weathermen and the Black Panthers increasingly led the movement. The means we increasingly used to further our cause included dishonesty, depriving others of their right to speak, destroying others' property and, eventually, taking others' lives. In order to silence our consciences, many of us in the anti-war movement came to believe that our highly moral ends justified the increasingly immoral means we were using. After all, our cause was just, so what did it matter how we achieved it?

At my school, student rioting began in February 1970. Over the next year and a half student unrest required the presence of the National

Guard on several occasions. I spent some time in the local jail and most of my freshman and sophomore years were spent planning and participating in antiwar activities rather than academics. I learned how to make a Molotov cocktail and how to crawl through the National Guard lines to toss it into a bank or an opposing attorney's office.

As the year progressed, I learned how to lie flat on a roof and shoot the police car windows out with a lead fishing weight hurled from a wrist rocket. I learned how to trash windows, shout down opposition speakers and close down a street or building. I learned how to get the attention of television cameras and how to make our side look like the victims to the press. I also learned how to incite a crowd to property crimes and violence.

We ate, slept and breathed the "Movement." I recall one day when I went off to a local park to relax and upon my return, I was harshly criticized by my comrades for being *counter-revolutionary* because I had wasted my time in the pursuit of trivial relaxation. Ditto for anyone caught smoking dope during revolutionary hours. The most radical leaders of the movement were beginning to make Richard Nixon look like Santa Claus and I began to long for my childhood days.

We radical students did permit ourselves one anti-capitalistic activity during our "off revolution time." We would lead food raids on the student union cafeteria. Several students sitting out on the quadrangle would yell, "Rip-off," and head toward the cafeteria. By the time we arrived at the food we were several hundred strong. We would fill up our trays and then walk right past the cashiers, as if they didn't exist. It was impossible to stop hundreds of students ripping off food at the same time so the cashiers just sat and watched.

In May of 1970 the anti-war movement received what many saw as a boost. Following the killings of four unarmed students at Kent State University by the National Guard during an anti-war demonstration in May 1970, the anti-Vietnam war movement exploded. Hundreds of colleges went on strike and did not reopen until the following fall semester. My university shut down and all of my classes were suspended the week following the Kent State killings, and I did not resume attendance until the fall of 1970. Considering how little time I had spent on my studies that semester, the strike was a timely reprieve.

During the summer break, I hitch hiked with my boyfriend to San Franciso, California. I spent much of the summer with a Buddhist monk. I spent the balance of that summer with radical students at various universities in California and between there and the Midwest discussing strategies for the upcoming year. I can therefore provide a first-hand account, including a few details that the pro-'60s revisionists have generally not chosen to bring to light

In September 1970, there were some minor skirmishes and some ongoing trials of friends to attend. Many of my friends had been expelled from the university and the "peace movement" was pretty well in retreat and the "revolutionary" elements were calling the shots. The leadership increasingly chose bad behavior, such as fire bombings and plastic explosives, trashing buildings, disrupting classes, burning police cars and shouting down opposition speakers on campuses.

Once again, I was young and naïve back then. So for awhile, in direct opposition to my upbringing, I swallowed with the help of much Pepto-Bismol, the flawed philosophy that the noble end of stopping the war justified the ignoble means we were now using. I hadn't lived long enough to realize what would become of the "noble end" when such immoral methods were used. I eventually learned that immoral means are not justified by ethical goals but rather they will defile and devalue the most well-intentioned ends.

One day, I was watching the news and saw a video clip of a group of anti-war demonstrators spitting on and booing a group of soldiers returning from Vietnam. I felt instant shame. My brother was in the Army at that time and might have gone to Vietnam. I wished I could have been there to reassure those sad-faced veterans. I realized that day that somehow, issues had become more important to us than the people we were supposedly fighting these issues for, such as our own soldiers.

Relative values conveniently allowed us to pick and choose when we were obligated to be honest, kind or fair. Further, since our lofty cause justified immoral behavior, it was no problem to humiliate returning soldiers who had kept their promise to serve their country and who had already been traumatized in war and now, thanks to us, again at home.

Years later, many veterans of Vietnam would say that the rejection at home hurt worst of all. I want to publicly apologize for my part in belittling the veterans of the Vietnam War and to offer my thanks for their service. I hope it helps them to realize that much of the abuse aimed at them by the anti-war crowd came from naïve and arrogant young people, many of whom now regret their words and actions.

Heckling veterans returning from Vietnam was not the only behavior that I began to find offensive. I will always remember the day I sat in an SDS cadre meeting and heard a "comrade" state that the killings by the Charles Manson gang were "a revolutionary act", as the victims were all rich and clearly part of the "bourgeois." The speaker explained that the words "helter skelter" written in blood by the murderers was a code expression for the very "revolution" we were all working to bring about.

The comment received a mixed response by the audience, as most of us were having trouble seeing the connection between Marx and Manson. At another "briefing", the bombing of the University of Wisconsin Math building, in which a professor died, was also noted to be a positive revolutionary act. Along that same line of thinking, it was a common belief that the more of our people who were injured or unjustly arrested during a demonstration, the better, as such injustices would "radicalize" or increase the militancy of the victims and sympathetic witnesses.

I remember feeling uneasy with the inappropriate excitement in the room when we gathered to discuss the Kent State killings and the opportunity that tragedy afforded us in furthering our cause. Where was the empathy and where was the sadness? The discussions in these SDS meetings never involved what we might due to help the victims or their families. These deaths were considered to be "collateral damage" in the war we were in, and the dead were thought of as martyrs rather than what they were--bystanders and casual participants in a demonstration that went wrong.

I looked up in one of those meetings and remembered the hopes for peace, love and tolerance that only a few years earlier had been the inspiration for our "movement" and wondered where we were heading and what we were becoming on the way.

In May 1971, I returned to Washington, D.C., for another demonstration, in remembrance of the Kent State deaths. By then, the Golden Rule and the belief that, "it's how you play the game," is important had been completely discarded for the less restrictive "me and my cause first" and "the ends justify the means" mentality.

Unlike the demonstration a year and a half earlier, this time we went to the nation's capital not to peacefully show our disagreement with government policy but to create a confrontation by stopping traffic flow on key streets, highways and bridges throughout Washington, D.C. We also assumed that this would lead to violence and mass arrests by the police, which would increase the media coverage and give us the opportunity to have our position heard nationwide.

I rode the 1000 plus miles to Washington, D.C., with about ten other students in the cargo area of a U-Haul truck. It was an experience that I am glad to say I never repeated. It was dark and cold inside the truck, and the driver in the cab could not be notified if someone were nauseous or needed to go to the bathroom. We didn't think to buy walkie-talkies which would have helped. In order to relax, we smoked pot and hash. We were in a relatively contained area and pretty soon the pot smoke got very thick. About this time we heard a police siren behind us and could see the lights flashing between the cracks in the U-Haul door. We found out later that a customer at the last gas station had heard our voices inside the U-Haul and notified the highway patrol. Our driver pulled over on an incline and when the police pulled behind us, our vehicle rolled backwards and attached itself to the front bumper of the patrol car.

As we waited for them to open the door, we heard quite a bit of cussing and threats coming from the officers. We used the time to locate and eat as many of the drugs inside the U-Haul as possible. When they finally opened the door and shined the floodlights in, the smell and smoke from the pot almost knocked them over. The head officer told the other one to call into the station and inform them that they had captured ten hippies that "wouldn't be making the demonstration in Washington D.C." After about an hour of threats and bad language, the patrol officers let us go. I doubt they wanted to process that much paperwork in one night.

We proceeded to the capital with no further incidents. I relate this rather humorous incident to remind the reader that despite the rhetoric of the day, the nation we were living in even in the late '60s and early '70s was still a free and relatively benevolent one. Most of us can picture how unfunny this encounter with the Indiana state police might have been in a true "police state."

After our arrival in D.C., we parked the U-Haul in West Potomac Park, along with tens of thousands of other demonstrators. In the evening, the Washington police and state patrol evicted us and we went to Georgetown University and stayed with students who would be participating in the demonstrations the following day. We rose before daylight the next day and headed out.

My "cadre" was assigned to the DuPont Circle area. We arrived at our appointed destination with our helmets on and tear-gas masks in hand in the early morning hours and prepared for a long and maybe dangerous day. The government, for its part, had also adopted the "ends justify the means" mentality. This became evident when the Washington, D.C., police and the National Guard seemingly decided that our constitutional rights were less important than preventing chaos. They gassed and arrested approximately 13,000 of us before the demonstration had even begun or a law had been broken.

That day, the government won the game of "Presumptive Reciprocity." This is a perversion of the Golden Rule which is sometimes called the ethic of reciprocity. This perversion directs us to do unto others first those things we would not want done unto us.

The police placed us on buses that transported us to the local jail. There they took our mug shots and fingerprints and tossed us into cells with 20 to 30 occupants. My eyes were burning so badly from mustard gas on everyone's clothes that I could barely see. However, I was able to identity one of the other occupants of the cell as my sister, who had come from Southern Illinois University.

Sometime that evening we were all released after paying ten dollars' bail. My sister and I and other friends hitchhiked home to Illinois, feeling ill-used. In fact, there was general outrage throughout the anti-war movement due to the obvious violations of our rights. In retrospect, it makes me smile to remember how angry we felt. I am not sure why the old expressions that we boomers had grown up with--*what goes around comes around; you reap what you sow and you live by the sword, you die by the sword*--never came into our minds.

I never felt the peace of mind and hope on this trip to our nation's capital that I had a year and a half earlier. I felt, or rather, I knew that somehow we were no longer headed toward that bright new land where brotherly and sisterly love dominated and people all got along. Rather, we were on the road to the dark places in human history where disagreement becomes paranoia and hate and, if it is not intercepted, can lead to the devastation of a society.

My limited 20 year old mind had seen for some time that we (the anti-war crowd) were not all that much different than our opponents. Eventually, my conscience began to rebel at the idea of heralding and promoting a lofty humane cause while disregarding the rights, welfare or even lives of real people in the process. It says in the Bible that I rejected at the time that "you can tell a tree by its fruit."

The rotten fruit of the anti-war movement's tree now included the taking of life, destruction of property, humiliation of others, ruining their reputations and depriving others of their rights. We were about as likely to achieve an ethical goal with these means as we were to get a tasty cake out of a receipt that called for old rotten eggs, flour and milk.

Although most of us were too young and impatient to see it at the time, in retrospect, it is likely that the anti-war movement lost much of its power and moral authority when we began using unjust means. We were lucky that by the time this happened, the majority of the nation had already turned against the war. Therefore the mainstream citizens and the media continued to pressure the government to end the war and the war came to an end, regardless of the damaged moral credibility of the radical anti-war element.

CHAPTER 20

Why?

In the beginning of this book we looked at a place in time where there was an attempt to control selfishness and promote the virtues of kindness, integrity, equity, etc. by teaching children about the Golden Rule and role modeling an ethical value system. Then society changed its message. Father knows Best was out and The Simpsons were in. Today, selfish behavior is not only ok; it is thought of as natural. So why fight it, hide it or apologize for it?

Predictably, the positive attributes that we have discussed, like humility, personal responsibility, honesty, kindness, fairness, remorse and forgiveness, went out the window with the Golden Rule. Among others, the attributes that tend to accompany the "me first" mentality are selfishness, jealousy, dishonesty, hatred, dissension, and greed. The quality of all of our lives decreases in a nation where selfishness is pervasive.

Over the years, I have been asked by the younger generation, "why" the baby boomers rebelled. Youthful rebellion and idealism do not seem to fully explain why a significant part of a generation raised to be patriotic, believe in God and live by the Golden Rule did a complete turnabout in a few short years, abandoning the faith and values of our childhoods. How did such excellent parenting in the context of a highly ethical society produce such a discontented product?

Dr. Tytler places "affluence" just before "selfishness" in the sequence of decline of a great nation. The 1960s saw the beginning of the greatest period of affluence in the United States ever known to mankind. The discovery of antibiotics alone greatly reduced the human suffering in our country. It was common to lose one or more family members at a young age to illness when our parents were growing up. The level of suffering that people endured just one generation earlier was almost unimaginable to the baby boomers.

Our parents had learned first hand during the depression how hard life can be and during WWII, how fragile freedom is. The baby boomers on the other hand often learned these things through historical, philosophical or ideological teachings. These sometimes black and white teachings combined with the growing affluence in our country set up unrealistic expectations.

I grew up believing that our country was indestructible. I believed that affluence, opportunity and freedom were the norm and that nothing could take them away from us. As time would tell, all of these things were not the norm but were really a gift from God paid forward by the sacrifices of many prior generations.

Our parents who were very good at teaching self reliance and responsibility were not the best communicators during the teenage years. Parenting techniques that were very good for young children can be a hindrance in working through problems with older children. When we became old enough to see that our parent's weren't perfect, we judged them with the same somewhat inflexible yardstick that they had used on us growing up. This was the other side of the coin to the "no excuses" we had been brought up with.

The civil rights movement and Vietnam only added to the discontent of a generation who had been taught that our nation could do no wrong. The beating of peaceful demonstrators in our own country and the rumors of massacres and killing of kids in Vietnam put the cherry on the sundae of our discontent. In our youthful self-righteousness and with the encouragement of the increasingly liberal media and entertainment industry many of us boomers turned our backs on the nation that had provided us with a wonderfully free childhood and the parents who had sacrifice so much to raise us.

When we threw out the values and behaviors that we had been brought up with we through the baby out with the bathwater. Our belief in the Golden Rule and our faith in God became casualties of the cultural war we had started.

Another factor that contributed to the *you-turn* we made in the 1960s was the natural hedonistic desire of human beings to live with minimal boundaries. Catering to the selfishness that is within each one of us, we choose as individuals to live lives dedicated to our own pleasure at a time when the opportunities to do so were increasing rapidly.

Like many of my generation, as a young adult I equated fun with no rules or restrictions. I realized that my childhood belief in the Bible was inhibiting me from engaging in all the available debauchery. When I tossed the Bible out I was free to try a variety of formerly off limit behaviors.

CHAPTER 21

The Trojan Horse

When the Vietnam War ended, the anti-war movement faded into history. As already noted, the values that had changed in our country, however, did not disappear. The emerging beliefs that selfish behavior was ok, that right and wrong were relative and that the ends justify the means were waiting quietly inside a Trojan horse sitting at our nation's gate. We young people in particular eagerly pulled it inside so we could share this *gift* with everyone.

"The Big Chill", the movie about the changes in the baby boomers several decades after the '60s, reveals how we Boomers became the people that we once vilified. After we spent the first half of the '70s resting up from our activist work, we Boomers began to gradually take over the reins of government, business, the media and most importantly, our kids' sports teams.

By the 1980s we had become the rich, arrogant, connected, image-conscious, materially-focused and selfish establishment that we had condemned in the '60s.

We then began showing everybody the meaning of a whole new group of anecdotes. "Me first," "might makes right," "money talks," "it's who you know that counts," "better you than me," and "the ends justify the means," replaced some of the kinder and gentler anecdotes that we boomers had been brought up with.

Although the new mentality first took hold in the baby boomer generation, some in our parents' generation quickly joined the quest for fun and self-gratification after Hollywood began showcasing the advantages of this mindset.

Many in our kids and grandchildren's generations have embraced self-centeredness with unprecedented enthusiasm, surpassing even their baby boomer parents. I heard on the news the other day that one out of five Americans are now certifiably mentally ill. The highest incidence of mental illness is in the 18-25 year old group (30%).This is no surprise as these young Americans are the first fruits of the new *me first* value system. (Reuters, 11/18/2010, *Nearly 1 in 5 Americans Had Mental Illness in 2009.*)

The truth is that acquiring more stuff, power, fame, etc., while ignoring our inner need to be loved and to love others, does not make us happy. There is an inverse relationship between happiness and selfishness. We derive purpose and happiness by being kind and generous and having positive relationships, not from operating as the Lone Ranger and stomping others into the ground.

The following discussion about the baby boomers' child rearing ideas and techniques, like our discussion of the WWII generation's parenting style, does not include everyone. There are many brave parents who continue to fight against today's strong cultural current.

The "me first" mentality is naturally causing enormous friction between people in every area of society. Everyone can't be first. The children of the boomers have been labeled "generation me." It's not a flattering label and it is not the fault of these young people that many of them have earned that label. Our children were being set up, even before they were born, to be self-centered.

Let's take a look at how the new "me first" and the "ends justify the means" mentality have affected how we baby boomers have raised these little extensions of ourselves and how their upbringing is affecting their outlook on life. The future of our nation depends on who these young people are and who they become. This is the generation that will either learn to work together to preserve our freedoms or they will continue on living out the selfishness that is tearing our people apart.

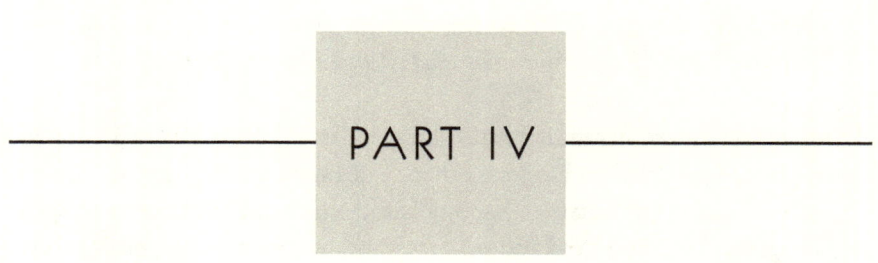

PART IV

The Young: Our Hope for the Future

CHAPTER 25

Our Precious Bumbles–to-Be

By the late '70s to mid '80s, the baby boomers began having children. This simple sentence in no way conveys the complex thoughts and planning that went into that decision for most boomers. Many of us spent more time reading child-rearing books and choosing a name for our as-yet unborn little protégés than my parents spent thinking about all four of their kids put together for the first five years of life. It seemed that the longer we waited and planned for our little bumbles–to-be, the more obsessed we were with them after they arrived.

With the help of birth control, most children of the boomers were planned for, waited for and eagerly anticipated, unlike my parents' four big, untimely surprises. This anticipation and preplanning, as well as the fact that many boomers chose to have one or two kids at the most, made the children of the baby boomers a highly valued generation from day one.

Many will deny that we boomers have as a generation been more obsessed with our kids than past generations. The day it dawned on me that we were a special generation raising an even more special generation was the day of my son's preschool graduation. There were more parent paparazzi on-site with cameras and video cameras for that event than at a presidential press conference. As I stood and watched those little three footers standing side by side with fearful faces alight with a barrage of camera flashes and video lights, I remember thinking first, "This is crazy," and second, "I've got to get myself one of those video cameras."

As parents, we boomers naturally wanted to avoid the perceived mistakes of our own parents. I have often heard my peers make comments like, "It hurt my feelings when"…or "My parents didn't make me feel special" or "They rarely told me that they loved me", etc. No doubt the WWII generation was focused more on survival and character development in their children than they were making their kids feel special. That is the way their generation had been brought up, and so many were maybe not equipped to be more communicative in their parenting style. They also believed that behavior and character were more important than feeling special and that if a person had good character, the likelihood was that self-esteem would take care of itself. Time would prove the merit in this idea.

I personally wish that my parents had hugged me more and told me that they loved me. I did and do hug my son a lot and tell him that I love him all of the time. That type of communication suits me fine. I also know that actions speak louder than words and that I count on my actions more than hugs or words to let him know how valuable he is to me.

Perhaps it is because the baby boomers grew up when children were clearly second class citizens that we have taken such pleasure in elevating our children to near-equal status with adults. I am only surmising this based on my own secret wishes as a child that I could have the power and respect of an adult. But is it really wise to implement the egotistical longings of a child once one is an adult? The privileges of adulthood come with responsibilities, most of which children are incapable of fulfilling.

Over the years, I have come to know that my parents and many of their peers believe that the baby boomers have facilitated and idealized our children in ways that society would once have considered bizarre and alarming. Unfortunately, most of us must learn from our own mistakes rather than from someone else's hard-learned wisdom.

CHAPTER 26

Baby Dearest

I don't believe that any normal parent likes to see their kid fail, be frustrated or have their feelings hurt. We boomers were a proactive generation and so we became proactive parents in attempting to prevent our kids from suffering from these things. Many of us therefore set about minimizing our children's frustrations, failures and serious challenges from the day they were born. To accomplish this, we have spent a considerable amount of time rearranging the environment and leveling the playing field.

Frustration was a particularly difficult challenge, as it could come from any direction at any time. Luckily, evolving technology was with us in our quest. Baby monitors appeared so we could immediately detect any movement or sound from our offspring that might convey a need that needed to be met. The microwave was another new timely technology that allowed us to fill up, heat and pop a bottle of milk between the little prince/princess' waiting lips within three minutes flat. I guess some of us felt that waiting a little while to be fed or picked up might hurt our baby's outlook on life.

Armed with current pediatric studies, we boomers felt that there was no point in having our toddler frustrated if we could remove the source of conflict. This did not just require the traditional removal of dangerous objects from a toddler's reach but the removal of everything we didn't want a toddler to touch. Why slap the little guy's hand and say, "No, don't touch," when you can simply remove the object? The answer to that question is "because then he/she learns not to touch it."

Childproofing our houses instead of house-proofing our children, as our parents did, has become business as usual for the baby boomers. In fact, by the 1980s, we parents were judging harshly those who did not childproof their houses, forgetting completely that prior generations were raised without this adaptation. Many of us even demanded that childless friends and family also childproof their houses.

My parents, who were in their fifth decade when most of their toddler grandchildren arrived, were not about to fumble with child hooks on their kitchen cabinets or to remove all breakable objects to accommodate a little non-taxpayer who they saw less than four weeks a year. So my child learned the word "no" early, at least at his grandparents' house. It took about three separate incidents of raps on my son's hands for him to learn "no, don't touch." I remember thinking how amazing it was that he seemed to understand and respond to the word "no."

Early childhood education specialists were our allies in the movement to reduce conflict, and they recommended confronting bad behavior, not the child. So we all began separating the child from the behavior. This is not a bad concept especially when dealing with behavior that may be beyond the child's ability to control such as bad habits or accidents. However, when this technique is applied to willful oppositional behavior it can be confusing. I sometimes wondered whether I had given birth to a child or a behavior as I seemed to spend more time chastising behaviors which had no ears or brain while my son sat safely on the sidelines, absolved of all guilt and interest.

Another new parenting practice that we boomers introduced was the habit of allowing our offspring to disrespect us verbally and sometimes physically. The experts encouraged this saying it would allow young kids to relieve their frustration by expressing themselves. "I hate you, Mommy and Daddy" became a familiar chant in many houses. At first I looked at this behavior as something like the overpressure release valve on a scuba tank. It was a necessary safety item that prevented explosions.

As time went on however, the damage this disrespect was doing to the parent-child relationship and ultimately to our ability to control our offspring became clear.

As time passed, many of us began wondering why our toddlers were so easily frustrated and so determined to have their way even as they passed beyond the toddler years. Our parental minimizing of frustrations didn't seem to be producing children with calm, positive and confident dispositions. In addition, the disrespect that many of us permitted our toddlers to show seemed to be growing worse, not diminishing as they grew older. Of course it did. These little short people were coming to believe that they were the bosses in their houses, not Mom and Dad. By the time he was two, my son had won every major conflict we had engaged him in, from breast feeding to scheduled bedtimes to spending time in his playpen.

The battle of the playpen was memorable. His dad and I were determined to win that one for the sake of our sanity. Following our very active toddler around all day was exhausting, and it also prevented us from getting anything productive done. We placed our little guy with a baby biscuit in one hand and his favorite toy in the other inside the contained area. He sucked contentedly on the biscuit for a few minutes, seemingly unaware of his new boundaries. He then began to look around and, recognizing his captivity and his inability to escape, he began to scream and the top of his lungs.

He interspersed crying, screaming, whimpering, and short naps from sheer exhaustion for several hours, until my husband finally removed him and folded up the playpen and put it away, never to be used again. For those feeling sorry for the little guy, let it be known that we followed the book and picked him up a hundred times to reassure him throughout that day. Nothing worked except removing him from the offensive pen. It was that or risk one of the neighbors calling Child Protective Services in response to the racket our son had kicked up. At this point we, the parents, were just beginning to catch onto the reality that our boy already knew. He was running the household.

We boomers have proved to be a strong generation, but not when it comes to our kids. When the time came for potty training our offspring, many of us caved in completely. Our wimpy approach to this developmental milestone set the average age for compliance back from 18-28 months to 36-38 months in one generation, according to an article by Baby Signs of Hong Kong. (*http://www.babysignshongkong.com*)

This article also states that it is actually easier and more appropriate to train a child before the age of two. By the time a child is over three years old, according to Baby Signs, the child has lost his initial discomfort with a dirty diaper and is more willing to ignore the toilet.

My mom had informed me that my oldest brother was potty trained by sixteen months and the other three of us were on board by 18 months. With more children and less money, my parents' generation could not afford to let us decide when we were ready to meet milestones, unless we were willing to use our allowance to buy our own diapers.

I was not confident in my ability to persuade my son of the benefits of going to the bathroom in a toilet rather than in a diaper, so I took up the task without telling anyone else. One cold California weekend, armed with a two pound bag of M&Ms and a book on potty training, I sequestered myself and my almost three year old son in the house in order to come to a meeting of the minds on the issue of potty training. At the end of the weekend, my son had diarrhea from consuming two pounds of M&MS and the potty training was put on indefinite hold.

I remember feeling like a failure because my son did not become potty trained until he was three. As it turned out, he was a regular Einstein in this area compared with the kids born ten years later. By then, most parents had bought into the idea promoted by the diaper companies, i.e., that kids should be potty trained when they want to be and not when they can be. The old Freudian fears were also resurrected and pediatricians warned us against pushing potty training too soon, lest it result in the development of negative life-long behavior patterns and personality traits. Since none of us wanted to find our son in a rocking chair dressed up like Mom, many of us got in line with the "when they are ready, they will let you know" mentality.

Pull-up diapers came on the market to accommodate this setback. It was a shock to parents when they found out that these pull-ups cost as much as a cheap pair of shorts and that four year olds tend to eat and inevitably void very differently than a two year old. The unholy connection between the proliferation of this new philosophy in child potty training and the profits made by the diaper companies whose customers now included four year olds was not made until a few years later, after the horse was out of the barn so to speak.

Predictably, this "let the child decide" mentality has leaked over into the territory of other mile markers. I know of two young children who have rotted out several teeth because they were permitted to drink out of a bottle until four and five years of age. I allowed my son to have a bottle with water and diet pop until he was three. My sister-in-law had to shame me into taking action by pointing out that "when a child is old enough to fix his own bottle", as mine was, "it is time to take it away!"

Not long ago, most students achieved a bachelor's degree in four years. Young people today tend to meander through college, dropping and adding courses, redoing those they failed and changing majors, with little care for the passage of time. Another mile marker, the average age that a child moves out of their parent's house, has gone from the early twenties to … I don't know, as many of us baby boomer parents are still waiting to find out the answer to this one.

CHAPTER 27

Lowering the Bar

Rearranging the home environment to suit our babies and toddlers gave way to "leveling the playing field" outside the home as our kids grew. Many boomer parents spent the decade and a half between our kid's toddler years and "adulthood" removing frustrations and generally micro-managing our kids' social, athletic and academic lives. Many of us have, through no small effort, secured for our kids the best teachers, coaches, schools, and social groups we could find.

A friend of mine was forced to approach her daughter's teachers so many times to keep her child from failing that we named her "Ms. Forrest Gump." We boomer parents have directed and done our kids' science projects and written their resumes and college entrance essays. Many parent's do not even attempt to hide the fact that they are doing their kids work. The third grader who did her own science project may find herself competing with a thirty-eight year old with a degree in engineering. As far as the schools are concerned, this seems to be ok because I have not heard of parents being confronted for doing their kids work for them and often it is very obvious. In fact, projects that clearly had adult involvement were often singled out for special attention and honor. When I was a kid, parents who did their kids' work were called "cheaters." Today we call them "involved."

We have lowered the bar so many times we would have to do the limbo to get under it. I have wondered over the years what message we send to our kids when we jump in so quickly to solve their problems or meddle in their lives in order to give them the advantages that they can't or won't earn for themselves. When I was a kid, kids usually solved kid problems. It gave us self-respect to experience the power of handling some of our own affairs. These days, so many parents are micro-managing their kids from such an early age that the phenomenon of "helpless kids" is widespread.

I see college kids who today who can't fill out their college applications, can't register for their own classes or keep track of homework assignments without the help of their parents. Frequently at lunches with my friends, one or the other will receive calls from adult children who need assistance solving problems they should have learned to handle many years ago. Sometimes I remember those long summer days when I and my peers traversed the city all day on our bikes, solving our own problems and making our own decisions without access to a cell phone. It almost seems impossible that we would have slipped so much in one generation.

We are often so obsessed with protecting our kids' feelings that we ignore the rights and feelings of others. A few weeks ago, I watched two small boys throwing and kicking a ball back and forth dangerously close to an elderly gentleman seated on a bench. Of course, eventually the ball hit the old man in the head.

The father of the boys, who had watched the unfolding of this little drama without interference, now came to the defense of the kids. He apologized for them and said something about them having bad aim because of their age. So he compounded his bad parenting by making a lame excuse for the bad behavior and apologizing for them rather than having his kids apologize.

Contrast the behavior on the part of this father and his boys with that of parents and their children in the 50s. It was the remorse of the kids and the determination of the parents to administer justice that eased the anger of the victims. In both situations described above, there is no justice, no remorse and no easing of anger.

CHAPTER 28

Self-Respect verses Self Centeredness

As part of our attempt to guarantee our children's happiness and success, we baby boomers have been determined that our kids would feel special. From the policy of giving trophies to all participants to the proliferation of "My child is the best little girl or boy in town," bumper stickers, the baby boomers have worked hard at making our kids feel confident and worthwhile.

My parents and their peers, who I believe loved us as much as we baby boomers love our own children, tended to let us know when we were kids that we were not the only pebbles on the beach. Conversely, we boomers have often given our own kids the message that they are the centers of the universe. Although we may not believe that our kids are the only pebble on the beach, many boomers believe that our pebbles are the ones that matter. How many fathers these days are coaches simply to promote their own kids? My son was in almost every sport, and I would say the majority of coaches today are looking out after their kids first.

When I was growing up, if you did favor your own kid on the team you coached, you did everything to avoid showing it. People's conscience generally prevented outrageous favoritism. A few years ago, I heard a Pop Warner football coach tell a parent that if the parent wanted their kid on first string, they could volunteer as assistant coach for four and a half months like everyone else.

Dr Lillian Katz, a professor of early childhood education at the University of Illinois, wrote an article in August of 1993 called "All About Me", based on the name of a pamphlet the schools were having elementary school kids prepare to increases self-esteem. (I prefer the word self-respect to self-esteem.) The article discusses the issues of self-esteem versus self-centeredness or narcissism. She points out that school programs promoting friendships would be far more beneficial to healthy development in children than the self-centered programs, such as the "All About Me." Sadly the schools did not listen then and these programs continue today encouraging kids to believe they are the centers of the universe.

Yes, our children are the ones that matter most to us, their parents, and it is not wrong to make our children feel special. To their parents, every child should be considered priceless. I will not deny that, as a child, I wished that my parents would hug me more and tell me how wonderful I was. However, this natural preference for our own children does not mean they should always come first, always get what they want or be taught that they are intrinsically (inherently) more valuable than others. To do so is a recipe for our kids' narcissism and interpersonal and emotional disaster.

Many boomer parents, in our attempt to make our kids feel special, have actually cultivated self-centeredness, dependency and weakness in them. It is often difficult to distinguish between self-centeredness and self- esteem especially when a child is young. It takes a parent, who is clear on the difference, to know how to encourage self-esteem and discourage self-centeredness.

As this younger generation aged, negative character traits such as jealousy, selfishness and immaturity persisted beyond the early childhood years. Now many of our children are in their mid to late twenties. Some have outgrown these behaviors and attitudes but many have not.

A fascinating book called *Generation Me,* by Jean Twenge, Professor of Psychology at San Diego State University (2006), gives us insight into these young people and how they think.

Her book combines data from many studies and confirms the suspicions that many of us have about the younger generation. They are very self-centered and are more likely to live alone; marry late, if at all; and raise children alone. The subtitle on the front of the book says a mouthful: *Why today's young Americans are more confident, assertive, entitled—and more miserable than ever before.*

CHAPTER 29

The Only Pebble on the Beach

Dr. Jean Twenge presents data from a study involving over 1.3 million school age and college students over six decades which reveals much about how this younger generation thinks and feels about themselves, others and the future. This study asks the current younger generation the same questions that have been asked of the targeted age groups for the past sixty years. The current age group tested includes the baby boomers' children and grandchildren.

The results are in and the younger generation, (better sit down for this news flash), is extremely narcissistic, according to the definition of that word. Using the survey "Monitoring the Future", along with many other studies and data from current students, Dr. Twenge identified seven traits associated with narcissism. She found that today's 14-16 year old group scored seven times as high on the narcissist's scale than baby boomers of the same ages did in the 1950s. (p. 70)

Narcissism is defined as a *pattern of traits and behaviors which signify infatuation and obsession with one's self to the exclusion of all others and the egotistic and ruthless pursuit of one's gratification, dominance and ambition.*

In his book *Malignant Love,* Narcissism Revisited, 2007, Sam Vaknin says, *They (narcissists) need excessive admiration [and] adulation; they feel entitled and are interpersonally exploitative and are devoid of empathy..*

Dr. Twenge says that the disturbing findings show that today's young people disproportionately have an inability to form relationships and worse, are aggressive when they have been insulted or threatened and they tend to have problems with impulse control. (p.78)

Let's see... " a *lack of empathy*", "*impulse problems*" and "*aggression when insulted...*" Is it possible that Columbine and its copycats have had more to do with narcissism than the spin the press put on it, i.e., "bullying" or "access to guns", for that matter? Not to say that bullying and guns weren't a factor; however, there's nothing new about either of them, whereas the widespread narcissistic personalities are new.

CHAPTER 31

Self-Centeredness Is Not a Social Asset

If self-centeredness led to happiness, this younger generation wouldn't be able to contain their joy. However, self-centeredness does not lead to happiness but to profound loneliness and depression. As Dr Twenge and Dr. Katz both note, there is a big difference between self-esteem and self-centeredness. The first involves good interpersonal relationships, whereas the second is about me being more important or special than others. (p 70)

When many of the young adults today do what generations before them have done, look to their opposite sex relationships and their friends for support, they often find that the self-centered worldview has no comfort to offer. The "me first" standard has effectively thrown up walls that prevent the loyalty, compromise and generosity that true friendship requires. How does a relationship work when both parties feel they alone are special in this world?

When I was a kid we often used the expression, "A friend in need is a friend indeed,"whereas today the expression that is more often appropriate is "With friends like these, who needs enemies?" I am lucky enough to count approximately fifteen young people, ages 15-30, of both sexes as friends. Several have given me advice on this book. These guys and girls are my nieces, nephews, children of friends and friends of my sons. Some are neighborhood kids. I have known most of them since they were born. It isn't hard to find out what these young people are thinking. It just takes an interest and a listening ear.

Not surprisingly, a popular topic with these young people today is the betrayals, disloyalty, self-centeredness and dishonesty that they have encountered. They often have very superficial relationships with their peers of both sexes and much of their disappointment is centered on this.

Specifically, the following issues reoccur in my discussions with almost all of these young people. They report that their best "friends" are not loyal or supportive. Rather these friends have most often been opportunists and are there in the good times but have are not to be found when the bad times came. Stealing each others' boyfriends and girlfriends was a social felony when I was growing up, but it is not uncommon today. One thirty year old son of a coworker just moved back home after a twelve year relationship broke up after he discovered his live-in girlfriend in his bed with his best friend. I can only imagine how devastating such a betrayal by one's girlfriend and best friend would be.

These young people also routinely betray each others' confidences, revealing private issues about their "best" friends to those who would use the information against that friend. Theft of each others' property and chronic "using" of each other for rides, money, social hookups, etc., are so common as to be considered normal.

I grew up with a give-and-take situation among neighbors. In other words, people informally helped each other out. It was a two-way street and no one had to be reminded of that fact. I have always tried to treat my neighbors as my parents treated their neighbors when I was a kid. In the present day climate of "get what you can", I have fed neighbor kids day in and day out for years without reciprocation. My son drove a neighbor boy to school every day for a year without being offered so much as a drop of gas by either the boy or his parents.

One neighbor boy routinely put in his request for groceries before I went to the store. He would then come over to help me unload the groceries so he could check to see if the requested items had been purchased. I know for a fact that my son never was offered more than a glass of water at that boy's house. I continued to be mannerly and hospitable despite such behaviors because I didn't want to "join them" in their behavior, and I hoped that maybe someday they would catch on. The results were mixed.

Lying to each other is rampant, even among the closest relationships. The lies range from exaggeration to pure fabrication. Once we took a neighbor boy snowboarding. The boy was unusually uncoordinated and after only one run and several painful falls, he took the board off and walked the rest of the way down and demanded to go home. The next day, the boy had put an extensive description of his (the boy's) expert snowboarding abilities and extensive experience on his social web site. Many would say that it was a harmless effort to save face however, in the 50's it would have been considered simply lying.

Although I enjoy their company and I find many of their insights fascinating, I worry about this generation. Many are profoundly lonely and that is the bottom line issue that we cannot as parents run away from. This loneliness at best diminishes our kids' joy in life and, at worst, leads to destructive behaviors.

We boomers love our children as much as any generation of parents before us. I know that some readers will be offended by the criticism of current childrearing practices discussed in this book. For those who have not followed the "me first" contemporary wisdom in childrearing, you have my admiration. There are also those who will say that there is nothing wrong with giving our children as much as we can and sending them the message that they are more important than others. These people often reason that the higher our kids esteem themselves, the more likely they will be to succeed, at least financially.

The fly in the ointment of that outlook is that the younger generation is suffering because their selfishness is keeping them from forming strong, lasting relationships with their peers. Getting along with others is not just an issue of personal preference. For human beings, it is often the difference between a meaningful life and profound emptiness.

Not surprisingly, Dr Twenge's data reveals that there has been a four-fold increase in young respondents who say that they are very lonely much of the time. (p.10). Twenge's findings also confirm that the younger generation has much higher anxiety and depression rates than prior generations and that this increases as they grow older. Suicide rates among the young today are also several times higher than they were in the '50s. (p.104)

Dr. Twenge also found that this generation was 30 percent more likely than their parents were to believe that outside forces control their lives and destinies rather than their own effort. She states: "These findings are very disturbing, because previous research found that young people with these beliefs are more likely to be low achievers in school, exhibit delinquent behavior, cope poorly with stress, and become depressed." However, their feelings of being more important than others and being entitled to success in life do not seem to diminish, even in adulthood. This sense of entitlement does not seem to be as tied to merit or accomplishment as it was in past generations.

Self-destructive behaviors such as branding, self-mutilation, drug and alcohol abuse and anorexia are common. This generation is literally going out of their minds from loneliness. Sadly, many do not even realize that life does not have to be like this.

When I ask my young friends who their most trusted friends are, more than half of those over twenty-five still say "my parents." What happens when we, their parents, are gone? Will this generation have to go through life as the Lone Ranger without Tonto? Will their pets be their only trustworthy support system?

Many, if not most, despair of finding another human being who knows how to give as much as or more than they take. They often admit that they are lacking in this area. How do you make a marriage or friendship work when both sides believe that they are entitled to get the most out of the relationship?

Most of them have or once had the same dream that young women and men of every generation have had. That dream is to become a father or mother someday, within the confines of a loving marriage. All of the material goods, expensive trips, activities and worked and oiled bodies cannot replace this dream.

These young people have a lot on their minds and hearts and I like listening to them. They have such a capacity to change once they make up their minds and can see the way. They will need that ability very soon as our country is spiraling out of control, economically, socially and spiritually. Like it or not, change is coming. Many young people have found the answer to our problems already, as we will see in a couple of chapters.

PART V

Bondage

CHAPTER 32

Apathy and Dependency

The opportunity and necessity for change is here for young and old alike. We must abandon our obsession with ourselves and our little groups and come together as one nation or, like many great nations before us, we will collapse into bondage. As we saw at the beginning of the book, democracies go through cycles of being born out of bondage, achieving freedom and affluence and then declining back into bondage. The beginning of the decline in Dr. Tytler's sequence starts with selfishness, which leads to apathy, dependence and bondage. We have discussed the impact that selfishness has had on our society and especially on the young. Now we will look at the growing corruption, apathy and dependence in our nation.

We don't have to look too hard to see the widespread apathy and dependency issues our people have. Somebody once said that in a democracy the people get the government that they deserve. Two statistics speak volumes about the level of apathy in our country. An A.C. Nielson study in 2009 revealed that the average American family watches over six and a half hours of television a day. Voter turn out in the United States has long been in the 60-70 percentile range in major elections and is much lower in minor elections.

Frequently I have heard people say that they do not want to hear about or think about things that are not positive. The economic collapse of our country is more than many Americans want to hear about. We generally prefer to watch our food and sports programs over engaging in an informed discussion of the problems we face as a nation.

Democracy must have an interested and informed populace to survive. Personal responsibility dictates that we be concerned about issues that don't directly affect us but that affect our nation as a whole. These days the majority of the time even those most affected don't take the time to get involved as new laws and court decisions continue to chip way at our Constitutional rights. To be fair, a good deal of the apathy comes from a conviction that we the people have no power to change the course of things any way.

A recent study showed that one in five Americans is receiving some sort of government subsidy. (Rasmussen 10/2010). Although many of these subsidies are legitimate and some have been paid into, it stills shows how dependent we are on the government.

The government will likely be running much of the health care system within a few years placing nearly everyone under the government's benevolent wing. More and more we Americans look to the government to solve our problems. This is the dependency phase of the decline of nations.

We often complain about immigrants who come to America and immediately sign up for some entitlement check. There was a time when immigrants came for the opportunities that our country offered. Perhaps some of the changes in immigrant's attitudes are a reflection of the change in our own citizen's behavior and values.

The following quote, attributed to both Dr Tytler and Benjamin Franklin describes what has happened to the United States.

> *A democracy cannot exist as a permanent form of government. It can only exist until the voters discover that they can vote themselves largesse from the public treasury. From that moment on, the majority always votes for the candidates promising the most benefits from the public treasury, with the result that*

a democracy always collapses over loose fiscal policy, always followed by a dictatorship.

We must avoid that dictatorship, especially in a day and age where technology has equipped governments to know everything about their citizens.

CHAPTER 33

The Return of the Radicals-
A Flashback to a Bad Trip

When I graduated from college, I left behind what I considered to be the old, failed socialistic politics and I assumed others did too. I had been turned off by the arrogance of a small group of people who believed that they had the right to impose that political philosophy on the rest of the nation without consent and by just about any means deemed necessary. The true nature of this mentality is "tyranny" regardless of what one calls it.

About fifteen years ago I began hearing and reading about ideas that were a flashback to my old radical days. I was hearing them from my son, who was bringing them home from his middle school and high school classrooms. A few years later these half-baked ideas became the norm in my son's college classrooms. It might have been amusing, but the proponents had not gained much of a sense of humor since the '60s and they meant business, as anyone who opposed them or their agendas found out quickly enough. I watched my son write papers spouting the professor's often very odd leftist liberal viewpoint in order to passa class. I haven't missed the irony that a one-time member of the SDS would be disturbed by in-classroom indoctrination.

I realized then that the small but determined group of anti-American politicos, some of whom I had known, had never left the campuses. In fact, they had metastasized to the high schools and middle schools.

Through the ensuing years, the ideological remnants of the '60s have gained enormous influence over the major media outlets. With the cooperation of those outlets and with the help of the censorship that is part of political correctness, these leftists now control much of the exchange of information in our nation.

Those of us who do not have a burning need to amass power and tell others what to do have spent the past four decades working, having fun and raising families. While we were attending our kids' athletic competitions and watching the Food Channel, these ideologues have focused their attention on gaining power over the rest us and have finally clawed their way to the pinnacles of power in our nation.

I know these people and how they think. In the '60s they were the outsiders, so they used guerilla-type tactics to attack the establishment. Now they are the establishment and so they use lies and divide and conquer tactics to extend the government's power over the people. Above all, they are arrogant and selfish, as are those very powerful people who have supported and promoted them. They believe that we the people don't know what's good for us and that their job is to impose their view of what is good on us. Our obsession with meaningless television shows and our ostrich mentality serves to convince these arrogant ones that we are a nation of sheep waiting for a leader to guide us from cradle to grave.

It is not a difficult thing for those who do not believe in democracy anyway to destroy the freedom of millions. In the 60s we shouted opponents down and intimidated them until they left campus. Today political correctness and the government mouthpiece, the mainstream media, suppress opposing voices. Would-be tyrants do not want intellectual competition.

Some may find it hard to believe that such a small number of determined politicos could by themselves bring our country to its knees. In reality there are other more powerful players in the game. Those that support these ideologues also tell them what to do. It is these richest of the rich that set the agenda for the nations of the world. They want more and more power for a variety of reasons. Part of their plan involves political and economic globalization. To accomplish that, they must destroy democracy and national sovereignty throughout the world. What is happening in our country is happening all over the world, and what used to be the bailiwick of "conspiracy nuts" is now openly discussed by the leaders of the world.

In November 2010 Nigel Forage, the head of the UK Independent Party and a leader in the fight against the EC (a first step in Europe towards globalization), addressed the unelected powerful commissioners of the European Union:

You are very, very dangerous people indeed. Your obsession with creating this Euro state means that you're happy to destroy democracy. You appear to be happy for millions and millions of people to be unemployed and to be poor. Untold millions must suffer so that your Euro dream can continue....because if you rob people of their identity, if you rob them of their democracy, then all they are left with is nationalism and violence. I can only hope and pray that the Euro project is destroyed by the markets before that really happens.

Interestingly, Mr. Forage was in an airplane crash in May 2010, which he miraculously survived. Whether you are for or against the European Union, the reducing of nation-states to dependent wards by that organization cannot be seen as a step toward freedom for the human race. In fact, the plan is not to give humans freedom as God intended, but to return us to bondage, as seems our fate.

CHAPTER 34

Bondage- Big Brother Is Coming...
Big Brother Is Here

It is clear that we have moved into the stages of apathy and dependency. Is bondage really just around the corner? Few would argue that our economy is in trouble. The debt that the government has run up trying to buy us off with entitlement programs is not payable and the interest is causing it to expand at a rate that is almost incomprehensible.

Capitalism requires a balancing act between the power and money held by the public and private sectors. As entitlement programs grow so do taxes. As small and midsized businesses go under due to increased taxes and regulations the pool of taxpayers shrinks and the pool of those on entitlement programs grow.

The Joint Committee on Taxation recently revealed that fifty-one percent of Americans do not pay income taxes, leaving the burden on the other forty-nine percent. The circle is complete as we must tax the remaining taxpayers more to make up for the losses sparking another round of small and medium sized business collapses.

Entitlement programs are easy to create but hard if not impossible to take away. People come to rely on them and in a recession or depression when jobs are scarce people need entitlement programs even more. In addition the money that is distributed through these programs keeps other industries going. If the government discontinues or reduces social security benefits, all of the industries where this money is spent, from grocery stores to automobile sales to insurance sales would be affected.

If we take away or reduce unemployment benefits, welfare benefits, VA benefits, active military pay or government retirement benefits it will have a profound effect on the economy. I don't know if our economy can withstand such a downturn long enough for people to develop other sources of income.

We are a formerly capitalistic economy which is now lopsided in favor of government control of the money and the power. It is the very, very rich who have control of the government. It is no accident that the bail out money went to the big banks over the small and midsized banks and actually increased the monopoly of the very wealthy families in the banking business.

So, what happens when an entitlement dependent populace loses those entitlements because the government runs out of money? We are currently printing money to temporality avoid the inevitable bankruptcy. However, the devaluation of the money that results from this has a bottom limit. When the money is worth next to nothing the chickens will come home to roost. The dollars days are dwindling and it is only a matter of time before its own devaluation brings it to an historic end.

The populace, with no means of self-support will rebel when their government checks are taken away. People must feed their families and there are no contingency plans to feed millions of people who have no income being made. Then the government will be forced to fulfill its mandate to *insure domestic tranquility*. Faced with a nation of over 350 million people, the majority of whom are struggling to survive; the government will likely impose martial law and suspend the Constitution. Historically, this is the beginning of bondage.

We desperately need a modern day Paul Revere to alert the people that "Big Brother is Coming" before the nightmare that we are no longer free becomes our reality.

At the end of the "Declaration of Independence" we read these well known words.

> *and for the support of this Declaration, with a firm reliance on the Protection of the Divine Providence, we mutually pledge to each other our Lives, our Fortunes and our Sacred Honor.*

As it turned out, many paid a high price for signing and defending that document. Now it's our turn to step up to the plate and defend freedom for the generations that come after us. As these courageous patriots did, invoking God's help and setting the bar high once again, let the boomers, the generation that accelerated our nation's journey towards destruction, spend the rest of our lives risking everything to help the younger generations put this country on the right track.

There is only one way to break out of the downward spiral we are in. We must denounce and turn away from the pervasive self-centeredness that is the root cause of our loss of freedoms and economic collapse.

If our nation is to do a U-turn away from the destructive path we are on, we the people must do a personal *you- turn* in our lives. The power to change our destiny has always rested with we the people and not the government. However, there will be great opposition from those powerful people who have a big stake in the way things are going. The powers that would rule us and deprive us of our freedoms are really just a reflection of selfishness taken to an extreme. They too need prayer and a change of heart.

Pulling our country back from the brink will be the fight of our lifetime. We cannot win with guns, guerilla warfare or by using the tactics of the government. They are too powerful and besides if we use immoral ends to achieve a moral goal, we and our goal will be perverted. We the people have access to weapons that are far more powerful than even Luke Skywalker's light-saber.

We must use the power of truth, the power of selfless love and the power in knowing the God of Creation and how He works in our lives to restore our country. If we are willing to leave some of our self-centeredness behind, we can know God and experience that power.

When God becomes our strength, things begin to change. God gave mankind free will when He, in all of His sovereign power, could easily have made us slaves. I think we can safely assume that God is on the side of our freedom to choose even if we lose.

PART VI

The Power in Truth, Selfless Love and Knowing God

---CHAPTER 35---

Tell the Truth

In the '60s, we in the anti-war movement were constantly looking for strategies to bring about the end of the war. Our strategies were not always honest, moral and in the best interests of our people. Today, our strategies for saving our nation must be all of these things. If we live out the Golden Rule as best we can, we will fulfill all three of these requirements.

Over the past fifty years our society has become increasingly dishonest. We must reverse this trend. The corruption in this country thrives in secrecy and with the help of the little people who do the mundane jobs that implement the agendas of the powerful. This means they need the cooperation of the average American worker, customer or witness. As citizens of the United States we must speak the truth. If only a quarter of the population just said "no" to dishonesty and exposed the dishonesty they see, corruption could not flourish and those who seek more and more power would have to emerge from the shadows and do their own dirty work out in the open.

If just twenty-five percent of the people told the truth about what they see happening in the military, in the government, in high places in industry, in unions or in the universities, etc., it would severely handicap those who use lies to gain power over the rest of us. It really only takes one brave, honest individual who is willing to risk their job, reputation, etc., and tell the truth to derail the corruption of many. A clear example of this is the recent collapse of the "global warming" intellectual monopoly after a few scientists had the courage to reveal the truth about the suppression of non-supporting evidence.

Just think about what would happen if the media would return to their calling... to report the news objectively. If just 25% of reporters and editors on all newspapers told the truth, the American people would be informed of the corruption and deception that has become business as usual in our nation. If the news station or paper you work for won't let you tell the truth, find another place to work or do independent writing, but find a way to tell the people the truth. There are many retired journalist and publicists that could start alternative papers without the danger of losing their jobs.

For those of us who are not in the media, speak the truth. Stand up to political correctness and yell, "The emperor has no clothes." The current socially imposed silence on many critical topics screams with dishonesty. The truth will shatter that silence and we could begin to have an honest discussion of our problems. This is what we must have before we can even begin to solve them.

JFK once told an audience of news reporters and editors that he trusted the American people to do the right thing once they were "informed." I believe that, too, but I know that we also have to want to be informed and take the time to be informed and to simultaneously demand that the media live up to their mandate to provide the objective facts and leave the opinions to the editorials and the people. We must have the courage to face the truth about ourselves our country and our world. We have been selfish and made mistakes. We need to stop compounding them by ignoring them. The courage it takes to face the truth is small in comparison with the courage it takes to take on a tyrannical government. If we meet the first challenge perhaps our children and grandchildren will not have to take on the second one.

CHAPTER 36

Living by the Power of Selfless Love

In order to pull our nation back from the brink, it is critical that we unite as a people. We no longer have the luxury of dividing ourselves into interest groups to obtain power, revenge or a bigger piece of the national pie. We have been seduced by selfishness, jealousy and greed into giving our allegiance to groups rather than learning to stand up and be accountable as individuals. As long as we are separated by race, gender, age, economic status, etc., our nation's problems will not be solved. We need to return to the individual accountability of the 1950s.

Governments should always attempt to bring out the best qualities in their citizens. For years our government has stirred the pot of bitterness and envy between groups for the sake of political gain.

Yes, there are grievances on both sides of most issues. The truth is that people are flawed and that is why God has commanded us to bear with one another and to forgive one another. Otherwise, it will never end! We cannot afford to wait until all grievances have been addressed between groups before we become a team and begin to look for solutions to our problems.

In his inaugural address in 1960, President John F. Kennedy said, "My fellow Americans, ask not what your country can do for you; ask what you can do for your country." He didn't address Americans as members of "a group" but spoke to us as individuals and asked us to put the common good first.

Contrast that with the politicians today, who at every whistle stop address a different special interest group with the same thinly veiled underlying promises: "These are the programs and policies that will benefit you and your group that I promise to deliver, paid for with other people's money, in exchange for your vote."

We are divided by our selfishness and we are getting nowhere in solving our problems, as the most powerful groups are constantly diverting our resources, focus and will to meeting their own needs instead of the nation's.

It has been a long time since the American people have come together, away from the shadow of special interest groups. Many felt a brief spurt of patriotism following 9/11; however, the divisiveness was quickly reinstated. Undoubtedly, there is comfort in being a part of a group. But true freedom, with its responsibilities and privileges, comes from operating as an individual. We no longer have the luxury of diving into groups. If we are to survive with our freedoms intact, we must return to a republic of individuals, where we individually take responsibility for our actions.

It is not the NAACP, MECHA, NOW, the AFLCIO, the ADA, or AARP, etc. that keep us free and prosperous. It is our nation, united despite our differences, utilizing the skills and efforts of all of our people, that must be strong enough and innovative enough to maintain the opportunities and freedoms that we have come to love and expect. How do we then get beyond these entrenched grievances and counter-grievances when even honest efforts to bring the truth to light are routinely distorted, resulting in more divisions?

There is only one way to break down the walls that have divided us for so long. We must love and treat each other as we would want to be loved and treated. When we live by the Golden Rule as individuals, the divisions will disappear naturally.

I once worked in an office with a black woman who had little use for white people and was very verbal about her belief that whites could not be trusted. At that time, one of my best friends was black and this angry woman told my friend to beware of me, because I would inevitably betray our friendship because whites "only pretend to be friends with blacks." I went up to this black woman and told her she was wrong about me. She was actually embarrassed, as no one had ever confronted her in the office. After that, I made it a point to talk to her. We eventually talked about many things. We got to the point that we could almost joke about racial prejudices.

I suspect that this woman had never in her life discussed racial issues with a white person, but our relationship allowed for that to a certain point. It was my willingness to violate the politically correct silence and to ignore the wall of her suspicion between us and reach out in friendship to another human being that chiseled a brick or two out of that wall. I don't believe our relationship erased her distrust of white people in general, but she did come to believe that there was perhaps at least one white person she could trust and perhaps her distrust of other whites was just a little less.

It is possible to break down the walls between groups, but there is a risk. Someone may hurt our feelings or vilify us in front of others. Considering what is at stake, I think it is a risk worth taking. As we break down these walls between groups, the destructive, self-serving, race baiting special interest spokespersons that claim to represent these groups will be exposed for the charlatans that they are. Then they will be free to find honest work or join many others in the unemployment line.

So how do we, who are being swept along in a raging river of cultural relativism and self-centeredness, somehow do an individual you-turn and head in the other direction, toward a life based on the Golden Rule? Is it even possible? Even if some people are strong enough to fight the current, how many can do so and how far can they get?

Perhaps we need an organization to facilitate this change. Do we need to begin signing people up for SPA (selfish people anonymous) groups?

No! Nor do we need people to WASP (work a selfless program) in an attempt to change our attitudes and behaviors. We need something far more powerful and yet far more simple than a program or government agency or czar. We need *an extreme makeover of the human heart, one by one,* similar to that of Ebenezer Scrooge, the Grinch in *The Grinch Who Stole Christmas* or Paul, the apostle on the road to Damascus.

What I am proposing is not easy, unless God leads us. Our country today is failing economically and this is getting people's attention. However, we fell spiritually long ago. The people in the 1950s were not perfect and many were not believers. However, because the society actively backed the Golden Rule, it made it far easier to live by it believer or not.

Today, we will need more than self-discipline to love each other or even like each other. The Bible says "I will put my law within them and write it upon their hearts." Jeremiah 31:33-34 NIV. When God performs this miracle, loving one another as we love ourselves becomes possible.

CHAPTER 37

Gods Love Transforms Us

No one exemplifies "selfishness" more than Ebenezer Scrooge, the grumpy miser in Charles Dickens' much loved story, *A Christmas Carol*. Scrooge's selfishness at the beginning of the story is only surpassed by his unhappiness. At the beginning of the story, townsmen come to see Ebenezer Scrooge on Christmas Eve and attempt to coerce or shame him into contributing money for the poor, who in Dickens' time, were poor despite extreme efforts to pull themselves out of poverty.

After he undergoes an extreme makeover of his heart, he freely gives to those in need. Laws or social pressure are not needed for Scrooge to be generous once he has had a supernatural change of heart. It is the realization that life is more than being a good businessman and the fear of dying alone that has turned Scrooge around. It is the realization that giving to others gives our lives meaning and is the basis for happiness that keeps him from returning to his old self.

The evidence of the extreme makeover of Scrooge's heart is, of course, partially the good deeds he does after his transformation. But even more so, the inner miracle is displayed in his eyes, his smile and his laughter. He is truly and completely happy, maybe for the first time in his life, because he has discovered the secret that God made us so that we would love Him and one another and that therefore it is more blessed to give than receive. He has exchanged his selfish heart for a selfless one. It is this profound change or you-turn of our hearts which leads to the change of behavior that we need to change the world.

Most people can agree that living by the Golden Rule will improve and perhaps rescue our society. We have all seen the power for change that extraordinary people living by the Golden Rule, like Martin Luther King, Abraham Lincoln, Gandhi and Mother Theresa, have demonstrated in their lives.

But does the average person ever undergo a true extreme makeover of their heart? Is there such a thing as a Scrooge-like transformation, or is it just a fantasy? After all the "heart" we are referring to is a metaphor. We cannot even see the heart we are talking about, so how can we change it? If there is no true transformation, then we would be better to put our energy into the old methods of bringing about change, such as waiting for our elected officials to pass laws and change policies, for without a true transformation, there is no power to go up against the raging river.

We will need an extreme makeover of our own hearts and a never-ending flow of love from God in order to prevent the cares and cruelty of this world from dragging us down into that raging river. So how do we gain access to this love? The Bible says God's love is always upon us. It's just that we must have a relationship with God in order to be aware of it. When we know Him, we feel His love.

The transformation of the human heart is a miracle, and it takes place one heart at a time, when an individual experiences unselfish love. Unselfish love comes from God, and those who receive it are commanded to "pay it forward" to others. When one is truly overflowing with God's love, the command is not necessary, as sharing that love becomes a burning desire.

1 John 4:7- *Beloved, let us love one another, **for love is from God**; and everyone who loves is born of God and knows God.*

I John 4:11-12 *Beloved, **if God so loved us**, we also ought to love one another. No one has beheld God at any time; if we love one another, God abides in us, and **His love is perfected in us.***

It is the unselfish love that people receive that causes them to be transformed. In the Bible this type of love is called "agape" love. It is a selfless, unconditional love that enables us to live by the Golden Rule...to forgive, be patient, be faithful, have mercy, and be kind, understanding and loving.

Love is for everyone. Forrest Gump said, "I am not a smart man, but I know what love is." He certainly did and in that way he was wise beyond much of humanity. The Bible talks about God and His love for us and the supreme position that love holds in God's plans. The Bible goes so far as to say, "God is love."

Since God is love and He is also the source of love, rather than "trying" to generate love within ourselves for others, we need only be a conduit for God's love to pass through us to others. We don't have to worry about getting it back or running out. By accepting God's unending love for us, we become filled with an endless supply of love for others. We can then pass it on in word and deed to as many people as we can, every day of our lives.

The following words from the Bible describe the importance of love to God and the kind of love that God offers and the kind of love He wants us to have for Him and one another. Reflecting on these words in the morning can help us live by the Golden Rule each day:

I Corinthians 13:1-8 NIV

¹ Though I speak with the tongues of men and of angels, but have not love, I have become sounding brass or a clanging cymbal. ² And though I have the gift of prophecy, and understand all mysteries and all knowledge, and though I have all faith, so that I could remove mountains, but have not love, I am nothing. ³ And though I bestow all my goods to feed the poor, and though I give my body to be burned, but have not love, it profits me nothing.

⁴ Love suffers long and is kind; love does not envy; love does not parade itself, is not puffed up; ⁵ does not behave rudely, does not seek its own, is not provoked, thinks no evil; ⁶ does not rejoice in iniquity, but rejoices in the truth; ⁷ bears all things, believes all things, hopes all things, endures all things. [8] Love never fails.

Passages such as these make it difficult to conclude that there is ANYTHING that God is more concerned with than love. It is His pure love that inspires and directs the extreme makeover of the human heart. The truth is that when even the most hardened individual consciously experiences the unconditional love of God, it changes them from the inside out.

The love of God can heal every diagnosis in the psychiatric handbook, including narcissism. It can take every division between our people and replace them with a sense of unity as we come to realize that we are all God's children and all the objects of His love. It can take the personal baggage that we have carried for years and transform it into a tool to aid us in helping others heal.

What we are really talking about here is changing a selfish nature into a giving nature. This is exactly what happened to Scrooge and the Grinch and Paul, the apostle. I admit I have never encountered a "ghost of Christmas" or a "Who down in Whoville," but I have seen this extreme makeover of the human heart over and over again in real life. I have also seen it in the mirror.

CHAPTER 38

God's Love is Performing Miracles Every Day

Human beings are transformed from the inside out every day. I have known hundreds of people who have undergone a change of heart such as Scrooge did. We will look at just a few.

There is a man who grew up being beaten by his father and watching his mother be abused. The man went to Vietnam after almost killing another young man in a fight, and learned to hate even more as he watched his comrades die. More than anything in the world, this man hated his father and fantasized about killing him.

When the man married, he began to be violent with his own wife. She and his children made plans to leave him, and he was considering murdering them. He had loaded his rifle and was waiting for them to return from church when a man came on the television talking about the need to be "born again." He felt like the man was talking directly to him and he fell on his knees and asked Jesus into his heart. That day he began to get well from the inside out.

Today this man is pastor of a church that has between 12,000 and 14,000 attendees every week. He began a series of outreaches is 1993 that have had over 340,000 attendees. The outreach is aptly called "Somebody Loves You."

Earlier this year, I met a lady who was in her late 50s. We began talking about our lives and she told me her story. She grew up with physical and sexual abuse in her family and her only support system as a child was violent gangs. She began to use drugs at nine years old. She lived a life of drugs and crime for three decades. She attempted suicide twice before she was 20. One attempt followed a gang rape.

One day, while she was on drugs, her unsupervised toddler burned himself on the stove. The child was removed from her custody and with him went the only love she had ever felt. Not long afterwards, she saw and heard the message of God's love on television. She asked Jesus to become her Lord and Savior and that day she felt the weight of her crimes and past life lift. She knew she was free to be a different person.

Before I even heard her story, I noted how she freely hugged and put her arm around people. She radiated love and happiness. She was quick to smile and her eyes were bright with interest when she was listening to others. Her words were generous with encouragement and her thoughts were positive. Her ways made people feel special when her attention was on them. I watched several individuals who seemed to be alone at this party walk over to this woman and shortly they, too, would be smiling and laughing.

Of all of the people at the party, this woman was probably the least physically attractive and had the least money and education. Her face revealed the hard life she had lived. She had many wrinkles and scars and looked older than she was and she carried a little extra weight.

Yet, judging by the facial expressions and amount of time others spent in her presence, she was the most popular person there. She knew what people needed as she did not withhold it. Her own suffering was the preparation that gave her the desire and the ability to ease other's pain. Near the end of the evening, she showed me a recent picture of herself riding her Harley with a group of ex-gang members from her church.

There is a saying, "You can't give what you never got." Many transformations have taken place in the hearts of people who have received no or very little love. However, they are pouring out love to others every day because God has filled them with His love.

The next story I am going to tell is one that should bring great hope to today's parents. Too many of our young people are in trouble with drugs, alcohol, depression and hopelessness. But I have good news. As frequently happens, when mankind strays too far from God's intentions for us and we experience the darkness which exists outside of the light of God's will, we are often desperate to come home to our Father. However, we sometimes need a light left on so we can see our way back.

An NFL star was expelled from playing football for using cocaine. This man believed his life was over, as all he ever wanted was to be a pro football player. However, God had other plans. This man had two Christian friends on his football team who came alongside him and began praying for and ministering to him. They brought him to a local church, and there he accepted Jesus as his Lord and Savior. God performed an extreme makeover of his heart and gave him a special calling to reach out to the young. I met him 24 years ago when he came to teach a Bible study of five people at my workplace.

Approximately nine years ago, this man left the church he was assisting as and went out to start his own church. The church that this young man started about nine years ago has grown to 12000+ and is listed as the fifth fastest growing church in the United States. The church is wonderfully diverse, with every race, age, educational and economic group represented. The church is an example of what we can do together once the walls that divide us are down.

A wonderful development in this church is that the most numerous age group is the under thirty group. This age group has traditionally not attended church. They are eager to attend this church. They are so desperate for trustworthy and loving relationships, as well as firm standards of right and wrong, that they quickly become regulars. For many the word desperate does not even come close to conveying the need they have to find meaning and love.

Judging from their testimonies and appearances, many of these young people are ex-gang members, ex-drug users, teenage mothers, and many have spent time in jail or juvenile hall. Others are college kids or young married couples. I have brought several young people to this church. Almost all are pleasantly surprised on the first visit, as they had believed that they would be judged, not accepted or encouraged.

Initially many are attracted to the caring, giving relationships within the congregation.

For some, it is the first time they have felt valued for who they are, rather than having to perform or play games to impress people. For others, it is the first time they have been told and showed that we overcome the loneliness and selfishness not by taking care of our own needs but by caring about others. Another lesson that they learn quickly is that love isn't primarily about words. It is about action.

After these young people have come to services a few times and heard what God says about these matters, they come to realize that the real power that fuels these changed hearts and caring, honest relationships is God's love.

Thousands of these kids go to church two to three times a week on their own to hear the Bible taught for over an hour because they want to, not because they have to. They go alone or with friends because their hearts tell them they have found the truth, and this truth gives their lives the meaning that material things and a selfish value system never did.

Jesus said, "I am the Way the Truth and the Life." Thank God that there is a Truth that sets us free and that this Truth is the most wonderful truth possible, i.e., that God, our Father and Creator, is love and that He loves us and has created us with the primary purpose of passing that love on to others. Jesus was God's gift of love to us, for "greater love hath no man but that he lay his life down for his friends."

As these young, insecure, lonely individuals experience God's love as manifested through His followers and submit to His authority, that love gradually removes the selfishness, insecurity, fear, confusion, anger, and jealousies and replaces them with understanding, forgiveness, courage, patience, purpose and, most importantly, a great love for others. When they experience, some for the first time, a true love for others and answer the call of that love, to sacrifice their time, resources, talents, and hearts on behalf of others, they find meaning and self-respect. The transformations taking place in this church are exactly what we need to save our nation, our kids and ourselves.

Recently a close friend of mine died at 53. We had seen each other almost every day for the past 14 years. She was an athlete, and her death from leukemia occurred within two months of diagnosis. She was a strong Christian and so, although she suffered and although she had two boys, ages 19 and 20, who would be left behind, she faced her death with courage and peace. She never showed a loss of faith or bitterness. Her friends stood beside her and went with her as far as we could. Then we let her go and, as John did for Jesus on Mary's behalf, at the foot of the cross, we promised to take care of her boys.

Since her death three years ago, one boy entered the Marines, got married and has a beautiful little girl. The other one, who had been messing with drugs when his mother died, took a few years to work through his demons. One scary night I had to take his loaded pistol from him before he harmed himself or his brother. Eventually, the memory of his mother's quiet faith and her friends' daily prayers for this young man took hold. He became a different person, almost overnight. As his anger left, it was replaced by a love of others.

Today, this young man is a blessing to our family and to all who come around him. He goes to church regularly and dedicates himself to helping others. When he goes to church, he tucks his mom's old Bible that contains hundreds of handwritten notes under his arm. He is at peace with himself and his mother's memory.

Just before she died, his mother told me that she was willing to give up even her life if it would save this son from his self-destruction. I don't believe God would take my friend's life in exchange for her son's, but

God promises to "work all things together for good for those that love him and are called according to His purpose" (NIV Romans 8:28). Truly, with God's help my friend achieved a victory against the greatest odds.

These "miracles" are happening one person at a time, day in and day out, in this church, in African huts, in Chinese homes and in hundreds of thousands of other places all over the world. Wherever the Truth is told, human hearts recognize and gravitate to it. That Truth tells us that we are here to experience the presence and love of God and to love and be loved by others. God set it up that way.

The examples I have given may seem extraordinary but they are really very common. Everyone doesn't start a church that grows to 12,000 in nine years. However, everyone who undergoes such a transformation has their own miracles to report. Even I do. When such a miracle does occur, it is contagious. It touches everyone who comes in contact with the one who has received and passed on the love of God.

I have personal knowledge of the individuals in these last two examples before and after their radical transformation, and I can testify that this transformation in both of them has been every bit as profound as was Ebenezer Scrooge's. From my point of view, these and the hundreds more I have witnessed are truly miracles. Seeing daily what God is doing in people's lives is a big boost to my own faith. Every day God shows himself to me in the love of others and in the love he has given and gives to me. The following is a synopsis of the road to and the road since the extreme makeover of my own heart.

CHAPTER 39

My Own Extreme Makeover

Like many of my generation, I came out of the '60s and into the mid-70s a changed person. I had left behind innocence, naïveté and idealism. I had also lost my faith in God.

I was beyond any illusions that our government was the squeaky clean entity that those in authority had once taught me. The emergence of Watergate eliminated any lingering belief I had in the moral superiority of the United States government. My conclusion about the politics of the '60s was that both the radicals of the '60s and the government had often behaved badly. I didn't hold any grudges, and I was ready to move on.

I believed everyone was out to get what they could for themselves and in reality, more and more people were living by the "me first" philosophy. I had believed in God as a child, but as I grew up and studied Eastern religion and humanism, I lost my childhood faith. My mind was stuck on, among others, the age-old question, "Why would God allow so much misery in the world?". I believed that until some questions were answered, I could not have faith in God.

I was not in the mood to search for answers, and so I set the question of faith aside for another day. Since I no longer believed in God, I was no longer concerned about my behavior except in terms of man's or society's rewards and punishments.

I graduated from college in the winter of 1973, and this terminated any lingering ties that I had with radical political groups on campus. I never wanted to pick up another political book or listen to another ideologue rant from the podium. I had more disdain for these groups than I did for government. I was now officially apolitical and looking for a little fun and relaxation.

On May 18, 1974, I married the man I had fallen in love with five years before, Lonnie Avery. I had none of the doubts or fears that many have when they get married. He was the love of my life, my soul mate and, in some ways, my teacher. The first thing he taught me was how to relax and enjoy life. He was from the lake country of Minnesota and we moved there for awhile after we were married. He played in a family band, and we boated, fished, skied and danced for six of the best months of my life. We were living a country-western song and I had always been a fan of C&W.

When I was with him, I was happy, regardless of what we were doing. When I was away from him, I missed him. Whatever the circumstances, if he was in it with me, I always felt that everything would be ok. We agreed on most things and we almost never fought. There wasn't anything worth fighting about, because we were both compromisers. Several of our friends allegedly got married because they were so impressed with our marriage. We went together like "peas and carrots."

Lon was simplistic in his approach to life. He was adept at living in the moment and avoiding the rumination and negative thinking patterns that I had developed. He was a college graduate but not a deep thinker, and he wasn't one to waste a moment on trying to solve anyone else's problems. He did not worry much about the future and he believed that the glass was half full, even when there was barely a drop in the bottom. There was one thing that we totally agreed on, though, and that was that the most important thing in life at twenty-three was to have fun.

We spent the next ten years doing just that. We hitchhiked throughout the whole country. Then we bought a red convertible Mustang and drove through it again. We went camping in every major national park, including the Canadian Rockies. We moved from Minnesota to California, where we made good use of our college degrees. In the recession of 1975, I got a job bartending at a submarine sailors' bar and he became the night manager at Der Weinerschnitzel fast food establishment.

Lon would get off his job at about two a.m. and drive down to the bar and help me get the remaining clientele out and clean up. We'd go down to the beach sometimes at 3 a.m. and eat cold hotdogs and drink Johnny Walker Black, an involuntary contribution from our jobs. Then we would sleep there on the beach.

We spent our spare time snow-skiing up in northern California, camping in the beautiful national parks and eating Mexican food with shots of tequila down the Baja. We boogie boarded all day and then drank tequila while sitting in the hot tubs in the evenings.

In the fall of 1975, I received a job offer for a professional job in Chicago. After a last kraut dog and bottle of Johnnie Walker gold, we quit our jobs and moved to Chicago. I had grown up in downstate Illinois, and Chicago had always been that big dangerous city to me. We were about to find out about Chicago's fun side.

My husband quickly got a job as an insurance adjuster, and we settled in the suburbs about 30 miles west of town in a place with a ski hill with snowmaking equipment, a pub, four manmade lakes and sailboats. The average tenant was a college graduate in their early twenties with a dog and no kids. We had volleyball teams, regattas, ski competitions and nightly progressive dinner parties at each other's apartments. We took up hang gliding at the Michigan dunes and attended the Indy 500 and Kentucky Derby. We threw sledding and tobogganing parties and acquired a hyper Irish setter puppy named Bridget.

After two and a half years in Chicago, we felt we had enough work experience to move back to Minnesota. So after a wild but sad goodbye party, my husband and I took ourselves and our U-Haul to Minneapolis. Wherever we went, we had fun. We rented an apartment on a large lake out in the suburbs of Minneapolis and bought a ski boat and put it in the slip right below our apartment. We water skied in the summer and rode motorcycles on the back roads in the fall.

Minnesota was a winter wonderland seven months of the year, and that was fine with us. We would gather in groups of five to ten snowmobiles and ride together through the beautiful woods and across frozen lakes into the heart of the wilderness. Then we would turn off the loud engines and build a fire and cook hotdogs and marshmallows on a stick. The quiet, snow-laden woods were so filled with spirituality that even an atheist like me could not ignore it.

When we were in town, we often partied with friends. This always included alcohol and sometimes cocaine. The problem with the alcohol and drugs was that, after ten years of increasing use, they were no longer optional. That is, if we wanted to have "a good time." They were becoming our master as all addictions do.

One time I had so much to drink I went over a small ski jump and landed face-down, dislocating my shoulder and biting all the way through my lip. As we waited for the plastic surgeon to come, I downed another beer with the uninjured side of my mouth. On another occasion we drank so much snowmobiling that we came close to hitting a car racing down the wrong side of a highway. At that time it was a joke. But that joke was getting less and less funny.

This shadow of addiction that was growing in our lives meant that we had slowly stopped seeing friends who didn't drink, slowly stopped doing activities that didn't involve drinking and slowly began drinking earlier and earlier in the day. We both knew we had a problem, but being young and amongst others who had the same problem it was easy to ignore it.

We lived our lives for ourselves and those close to us. The selfishness grew with the alcohol use and we began to seek other more out-of-bounds ways to "feel alive." We began shop-lifting, *dining and dashing,* and engaged in petty white collar crime. Once we drove into a drive-in-theater via the exit and then, when our presence was discovered, we almost ran the attendant down trying to get away. On one occasion, we hooked a large boat up to our car and took it 80 miles up the road before we dumped it after seeing a highway patrol go by. We didn't want the boat, we already had one, it was the thrill that we wanted.

At the time, I knew there was something odd about what we were doing, but I dismissed what was left of my conscience with the well used excuse that we weren't as bad as others. Looking back I realize that there was emptiness in our lives that we weren't even consciously aware of. We chose alcohol, non stop activity and committing small crimes to fill the emptiness.

There was nothing wrong with all of the hobbies and activities we had spent the last several years enjoying. But they alone did not provide lasting meaning. Neither did drugs or alcohol. We had thrown the only source of lasting meaning out when we turned our backs on God years ago.

Solomon, the man who was given wisdom above all things, spent much of his young life searching for meaning in pleasure, work and acquisitions. He found in the end what we all find. He found that without God there is nothing under the sun that provides meaning.

> *I denied myself nothing my eyes desired;*
>   *I refused my heart no pleasure.*
> *My heart took delight in all my labor,*
>   *and this was the reward for all my toil.*
> [11] *Yet when I surveyed all that my hands had done*
>   *and what I had toiled to achieve,*
> *everything was meaningless, a chasing after the wind;*
> *nothing was gained under the sun.*
>
> Ecclesiastics 2:10 NIV

Who knows where all of this would have ended up if not for the arrival of someone who changed my life forever? On March 24, 1982, my thirty-first birthday, I gave birth to our first and only child, a bouncing and determined baby boy that we named Erik. He was big and healthy as I discontinued all drugs when I decided to get pregnant and all but a rare glass of wine throughout my pregnancy.

Shortly after my son was born my husband and I split up. The day we separated was one of the worst days of my life. I still loved him and yet, for him, it was over.

I called my old job in Minnesota and when they hired me back a year and a half later, Erik and I moved back to Minnesota to be closer to family. More than anything in the world I wanted to be a good mom. I hoped that a new start would improve my mood and enable me to stop drinking.

Obviously hoping wasn't enough and soon I was drinking more and keeping company with a couple of guys. I felt cheap, weak and hopeless. I had had two serious relationships in California but my bitterness was a wall between me and any healthy relationship. I was totally empty.

Beyond the obligation I felt for my little boy, I had little interest in life. Each day was drudgery. I had no faith, no hope and no comfort. I reached the end of the rope that God had given me sometime during that first long gray winter back in Minnesota. I just couldn't handle the shortage of money, the boring job, the lack of many friends, the drinking problem and the lack of a light at the end of the tunnel.

I loved my little boy and for his sake, I got up and went to work every day. But what I wanted to do was to go under the covers and never come out again. I wasn't sure how long I could make it.

Then one day, looking out on that grey world, I noticed a spot of color. My sluggish mind did a double-take and after a brief delay, it identified the spot as my older brother. But something was different. If anyone fit into the gray in the past, it was my brother. Now he was a beacon of light, defying the gray and emitting a joy of life that threatened to send the gray day packing.

Suffice it to say, he seemed happy and at peace for the first time in his adult life. A few days later, I asked him about this change and he replied simply that it was having God in his life that had changed and was changing everything. I asked how I could get God in my life, wondering at the same time what exactly that meant. Even before I asked, I was already convinced that God wouldn't be too interested in me after He took notice of some of my shenanigans over the past several years.

Instead of a laundry list of "to do's" to get myself presentable to God, my brother told me to simply confess my sinful behavior and thoughts, turn away from them and accept Jesus' sacrifice on my behalf. This seemed like a long shot for an atheist like me. It was all too complicated. As time would reveal, I personally understood much less than I thought I did about God, Jesus, and faith.

Despite the fact that I occasionally went to church as a kid and knew something about the Bible, I was very confused the first time I heard about God's love and plan to satisfy justice as well as to show mercy through Jesus' sacrifice. It made absolutely no logical sense to me when I first heard it. How could the death of Jesus do anything for me and my relationship with God? Why did I have to acknowledge my sins when I wasn't any worse than anyone else? Besides, didn't God already know everything I had done wrong? What sense did it make to accept Jesus? Why was it a choice, anyway? Couldn't God just put Jesus in my heart? Besides, who ever heard of God loving us if we didn't do something to earn it? My rational mind went on and on in its protest and attempt to thwart the best decision I ever made in my life.

However, I knew that I needed to get my life together for the sake of my son, and I had traveled as far down the "me first" road as I could go. I stared straight into the eye of the emptiness that had dominated my life since the '60s and knew it for what it was...the emptiness of a life without God. I therefore repeated after my brother the sinner's prayer.

My "faith" was more of a hope, and I accepted Jesus into my heart with almost no belief that anything would come of it. The key is that I wanted with all of my heart and will for something to come of it, but I believed with my entire mind that nothing would. God, in His love, ignored my mind and honored my heart.

Sometimes, when we are empty and broken and don't know how to fix our lives or our nation, we need to listen to the longings of our lonely hearts and souls and boldly step into the non-material world of faith and spirit to find the answers.

CHAPTER 40

Peace

Shortly after I came to know Jesus and the love of God, a cardiologist informed me that my four year old son would have to have heart surgery. I was surprised at the peace God gave me about that. It was one of the biggest stressors I had ever faced, and yet I had peace about it from the beginning. Another change that I noticed right away was that God took away my sadness and replaced it with the joy of being a mom. I still have that joy twenty-four years later. My anger, bitterness and feelings of victimhood disappeared and were replaced by a sense of thankfulness that God had found me and had seen me through my wayward wanderings.

I am especially glad that God took my anger at Lonnie away. I had the privilege of leading him in the sinner's prayer before he died in his sleep at 56. I believe his heart was sincere but like all of us, his flesh was weak.

Jesus said, "I am the light of the world. Whoever follows me will never walk in darkness, but will have the light of life" (John 8:12 NIV). God brought a light into my life after many years of living in the darkness. Since the day I asked Jesus to reign in my life, no matter how dark the storms around me, that light is always there.

Over the years, God has been with me, changing me and guiding me. After the mustard seed of hope and faith grew within me in the first few years, I have never doubted His existence. He has proved Himself to me over and over again. As will be revealed in the next chapter, I have had failures. Yet there have been so many victories...over alcohol, over drugs, over attitudes and behaviors that I thought I would take to my grave. God works on the inside. Sometimes the progress shows on the outside and sometimes it doesn't. But I feel the change in my heart, where it counts.

---- CHAPTER 41 ----

The World is Still the World

Has my life been a "bowl full of cherries" since the day I asked Jesus to send God's Holy Spirit to live inside of me to guide and change me? Am I ready for sainthood after twenty-seven years of knowing my Redeemer? Not hardly! I am not perfect, nor is my life free of pain and sorrow. Christians have problems, failures, and tragedies just like everyone else. God does not "zap" us into being well-behaved robots any more than He made us that way to begin with. Changing into a more loving person is a process. We retain our free will throughout that process. Plus, we still are citizens of this fallen world until the day we die and therefore, we are subject to the tragedies and outrages of this world.

With me it's been a slow, steady change with occasional spurts and a few backslides. I have to say that the spurts have always been triggered by a challenge or tragedy. Many of us want instant change, but God in His wisdom likes processes. Processes provide the time and room for our free will to do a dance with His truths and purposes so that the end product is a joint effort. I recently learned a powerful lesson about where our strength comes from and the truth of the Bible verse I Corinthians: 10:12: "So, if you think you are standing firm, be careful that you don't fall!"

This happened over two decades after I became a Christian and at a time when, frankly, I felt I had grown beyond such undisciplined behavior. I fell into an obsession with gambling. I had never had a gambling problem and had visited casinos all of my adult life without a problem. Then I began taking a medication for my Parkinson's disease which I was unaware had a known side-effect that caused compulsive gambling, shopping, eating and sexual behavior. I was lucky enough to only succumb to the gambling and eating.

I had gone to casinos off and on since I was 21 years old. I would gamble perhaps $30-50 and then go to the pool or show, etc. My medication was up to four pills a day when my brother and his wife came for a visit. We went out to a local Indian casino just for fun. It was my first trip to one of the local casinos. After that night, I was hooked.

When my brother left, I returned to that casino alone. I went from a person who had had a better than 800 credit score for over thirty years to a person with bad credit and who was barely able to pay my bills. I ended up in bankruptcy.

I felt for a while that I could not call myself a Christian anymore. The only bright spot in my faith was that I never gave up my personal commitment to try to make time to do for others out of love. The Bible says "love covers a multitude of sins" and we know that Jesus gave His life to "cover" all of our sins. When I feel God's love and I pay it forward to others, no matter what the circumstances, I feel at peace and hopeful that God will give me victory over the sins in my life.

I know that the feeling of peace and purpose that helping others gives me kept me from giving up. I believe that is why, no matter how deep I sank in failure and shame, I always felt God's presence. When I say that loving people by our actions is more a gift for the giver than the receiver, I am speaking from first-hand experience.

So, despite the pain and shame, this episode in my life taught me once again that "we are weak, but He is strong." God also kept His promise to "work all things together for good for those who love Him." Romans 8:28, NIV. Because of my gambling, my heretofore dependent twenty-something year old son had to not only start taking responsibility for his own life but had to pick up some of the household financial burdens. This drove him closer to God. He has stepped up to the plate in every way and I believe he has grown spiritually and emotionally into a stronger, more kindhearted person. He, like I did, has found that sacrificing for others gives life purpose. I couldn't be prouder or happier for him, because he has an unshakable faith in God. He and I both know how much he is likely to need it in the world ahead.

My failures and hard times have been bearable with God there to pick me up, dust me off and tell me that He forgives me and believes in me. Some might ask what in the world I have to show for 22 years of a relationship with Jesus Christ if I can still fall into a sin like compulsive gambling. I would answer that God is teaching me many things, but foremost He is teaching me how to love others. Part of that is accepting that people aren't perfect and forgiving them. Part of that is forgiving myself.

In almost every way, even in failure, God has blessed me since I let Christ sit in the driver's seat of my life. The 23rd Psalm, which most of us are familiar with, beautifully describes a lamb's dependence on the good Shepherd. This is the way it was when God's Holy Spirit came to live inside of me. I was so desperately in need of green pastures, quiet waters and the peace that surpasses understanding in my life. As the years went on, I also needed Him to walk with me through the valley of the shadow as I fought breast cancer and now as I am in a battle with Parkinson's disease and a degenerative spine.

About six months ago I had over eight hours of deep brain stimulation surgery for Parkinson's disease. I am still trying to get the equipment and medications in balance. I still have many of the symptoms I had before the surgery plus a few more. However, God has given me peace. There is nothing else that medical science can do to significantly increase my quality of life. Life is a struggle, some days more than others. But things are so much clearer when I let God lead me. Truly, very few things matter to me anymore, other than faith and loving people.

Part of loving people is helping to get our country back on the right track. Not so we can all have more iPods but so that a 10 year old can ride her bike all over town every day of the year and not have to put a lock on it or worry about being kidnapped and killed. I want all of our children to grow up in a society that offers freedom and love, as well as the ability to earn a decent living.

God has done so many things for me. His love gives me comfort and peace as well as promotes endurance. The thief on the cross to whom Jesus promised Paradise got in just under the wire. Some consider that he did it right. He lived as he pleased all of his life and then was qualified for eternal life based on a last-minute confession. However, he missed the blessings of knowing God all of his life.

When my time to pass from this world comes, I know that He will walk with me through the valley of the shadow of death. He has been with me all of these years, so why should it be any different on that day?

If you let Him, God will do His own special work in your heart and life. It is this work that the Spirit of God does inside of us that will give us the ability to save our nation and its freedoms.

CHAPTER 42

A Challenge for Christians

For all of you whose hearts have already been changed by the Holy Spirit and who count yourselves as part of the "salt of the earth," this is an opportunity to do something for our nation and our kids.

As Christians in a more and more secular nation, many of our past efforts to speak out and participate in the political process have often seemed to be a waste of effort. Our objections to the debased cultural trends are belittled, distorted or ignored. Our efforts are marginalized and often vilified. Worst of all, we often find that our kids are being carried downstream by the powerful current of the same mighty cultural river that is defining our society.

It is little wonder that so many Christians have pulled back from a world that seems to want our input less and less. Many of us have retreated into enclaves of Christian friends and family members. We live lives dedicated to taking care of those we have chosen to let into our trusted circle.

However, as the nation we love, not to mention some of our children, are falling deeper and deeper into chaos and spiritual darkness, many of us feel a strong calling to do something about it. Yet, many of us also feel helpless. We have forgotten that within us is the greatest power for change that exists ...the love of God. We have the power in us, God's love, to turn this whole nation around and, in the process, to revitalize our personal faith and purpose.

What if we came out of our Christian cubbyholes and offered our love and hope to non-Christian strangers all day long? If those who have experienced God's love would pay that love forward to the love-starved world, we would see the greatest revolution in human history. We have already seen how selfishness is the common denominator in all of our problems. Selfishness is the bait by which we have all been ensnared into participating in the "me first" mentality that has poisoned every aspect of our lives. .

Put another way, God's love is the light that drives back the darkness. People who feel unloved or unlovable are the primary source of unloving behavior. When a person is snake bitten, we give them an antidote. We need to receive from God and offer to each other the antidote to selfishness…love.

If you know Jesus and have faith in the Bible, start living by God's commandment to love others as you love yourselves and you will see the world around you change dramatically for the better.

What would this entail? Love, as Jesus showed us, is a verb and it is best manifested when we sacrifice for one another. "Greater love hath no man but that he lay down his life for his friend." Love is not telling people that we love them. It is showing them that we love them. Christian love for our fellow human beings is displayed in a concern for others' welfare translated into a willingness to sacrifice time, energy, possessions or whatever it takes to meet others' needs.

There are opportunities to "give" all day long. Our gifts and talents, as listeners, counselors, problem solvers, encouragers and providers will likely be needed, depending on the people we reach out to. It doesn't matter if it is a smile, a touch or helping a neighbor to put a roof on their house. What people need is for someone to show that they care about them.

The mission field is our neighbors, our coworkers, friends, family and customers. We may reach out to a store clerk or a gas station attendant, a street person or a politician. There are prisoners in jail to write to and children in child protective custody to visit. Everywhere in this nation today, there are people hurting and in need of love in action. If you don't see them, it is because you are not looking closely. Pray to God to help you see the needs and I have no doubt you will begin to see them everywhere.

Those who take the challenge to go beyond their interpersonal comfort zones will likely find that helping others can quickly become addicting. This is an opportunity to do it your way according to your gifts, assets and vision and to fulfill God's plan for you while you're at it.

For Christians, this is a win-win situation. As we sacrifice for others we become more loving, and God will be sanctifying us as we sacrifice with a pure heart to show others the love that has redeemed, saved and changed us.

As others feel loved, they become more loving. Love leads directly to God and so as love spreads and multiplies, opportunities to share the gospel will abound and people will get saved. When we immerse ourselves in God's work, we regain meaning, purpose and peace in our lives.

So, my brothers and sisters in Christ, your mission, should you decide to accept it, is the same mission that we have had all along. It is to love God and one another. Out of this love comes the honesty, kindness, patience and all of the other fruits of the Spirit. It is a mission of joy and hope to our nation and eventually, the world.

I believe as do many Christians, that we are now in the times spoken of in the Bible as the time of Christ's return. This does not mean we should sit contentedly in our salvation and wait. Whatever God's timetable for His plan for the Ages is, we know that it is God's will that His people share the message of His Love as much as we can to as many as we can for as long as we can.

CHAPTER 43

A Message for Non-Christians

I now want to address the readers who believe in the ethics of the Golden Rule and want to turn our country around but don't believe in or follow the God of the Bible. Our country needs all of its citizens, regardless of their faith, to work together to rebuild our nation. Your positive attitude and loving kindness towards your fellow citizens will be a blessing to all who come in contact with you. The work described in the prior chapter is for everyone who chooses to join in.

Many people in the '50s did not have a personal relationship with God and yet they lived lives that were generally in keeping with the Golden Rule. It was certainly easier back then, however, when society was reinforcing that viewpoint.

My youngest brother is a great lover of people but he rejects the God of the Bible. However, I know he and his Maker will meet someday because my brother loves. Read the following passage from I John 4:7-21 NIV.

> ⁷*Dear friends, let us love one another, for love comes from God. Everyone who loves has been born of God and knows God.* ⁸*Whoever does not love does not know God, because God is love.* ⁹*This is how God showed his love among us: He sent his one and only Son into the world that we might live through him.* ¹⁰*This is love: not that we loved God, but that*

he loved us and sent his Son as an atoning sacrifice for our sins. ^{11}Dear friends, since God so loved us, we also ought to love one another. ^{12}No one has ever seen God; but if we love one another, God lives in us and his love is made complete in us. ^{13}We know that we live in him and he in us, because he has given us of his Spirit. ^{14}And we have seen and testify that the Father has sent his Son to be the Savior of the world. ^{15}If anyone acknowledges that Jesus is the Son of God, God lives in him and he in God. ^{16}And so we know and rely on the love God has for us. God is love. Whoever lives in love lives in God, and God in him. ^{17}In this way, love is made complete among us so that we will have confidence on the day of judgment, because in this world we are like him. ^{18}There is no fear in love. But perfect love drives out fear, because fear has to do with punishment. The one who fears is not made perfect in love. ^{19}We love because he first loved us. ^{20}If anyone says, "I love God," yet hates his brother, he is a liar. For anyone who does not love his brother, whom he has seen, cannot love God, whom he has not seen. ^{21}And he has given us this command: Whoever loves God must also love his brother.

These passages make it clear that "love" is the defining issue of our lives from God's point of view. If you truly love your fellow man, then you are with us and welcome in the battle.

My only plea to you, then, is to consider the battle. It is against a mighty river these days. It is a difficult thing to live in a way that goes against the mainstream current. It is especially hard to be a giver in a taker society. That is why those who intend to undertake to right the wrongs, to love their fellow man and live by the Golden Rule in their own strength should be honest about the challenges.

There is an old movie called *The Heart Is a Lonely Hunter* about a deaf-mute man who unselfishly attempts to help others who are struggling with loneliness and depression. The deaf-mute pours his kindness, concern and love into the other characters and into one in particular who is completely unable to return it. As time passes, the deaf man finds that he is unable to refill himself after he pours his kindness, concern and love into others. He does not have an endless supply of love or understanding, and so, his own reservoir of love eventually becomes depleted. In the movie, the deaf man commits suicide when he faces the reality of life's lonliness.

Most people are somewhat fulfilled when their sacrifices are appreciated and acknowledged. The appreciation seems to partially refill our cup of generosity after we have emptied it. But when people return our goodness with scorn and our generosity with thanklessness (and believe me, they will), our human pride tends to get in the way and eventually, our limited human love tends to fail. In other words, we grow weary of being "good" to those who do not appreciate it. Although we often wish we were better than this and we may see ourselves as very altruistic, I believe when most people search themselves they will see this is the reality.

So, we often tend to limit who and how much of ourselves we offer to others. Every day we all see and then turn away from people who have needs that we could meet. We often unconsciously conserve our time, money, emotional energy for those we care about. It's as though we believe if we give too much away, we will be depleted. This is a very real problem today in a society that often devours kindness in one gulp.

How, then, do we avoid depletion? As a Christian, my experience is that we must have our hose attached to the source of the water/love, which is God. That is why the greatest commandment has two parts. The first is to love God with all of our heart soul and mind and the second part is to love our neighbor as ourselves. The love we have for God comes from Him. We love Him because "He first loved us" (I John 4:19 NIV).

When we love others with the unselfish or unconditional love that God gives us, the love we give away will have less of the self-serving traits and conditions, such as jealousy, desire for control or fear of abandonment, so common in self-generated, conditional human love.

For those readers who do not have faith and have never experienced God's love, but who want to be part of a "movement" based on living by the Golden Rule, I salute your kind hearts. I do not intend to browbeat anyone. I will ask that you consider what has been said in the past chapter and what is being said here. I have great faith in the truth and I firmly believe that for all who undertake this calling, the love and truth of God will be revealed to you in God's own time.

If you, like every human being I have ever met, are searching or hoping to find eternal, unconditional love, consider hooking your hose up to the source of all perfect love...the God of the Bible. The work of living according to the Golden Rule in a "me first" society will be difficult, but with God refilling us, it can actually be a joyful journey rather than an agonizing one.

CHAPTER 44

Receiving God's Love

There is so much misinformation out there about Christianity and Christians that it is hard even to know where to start...with a statement or with an apology. I am not attempting to "convert" anyone, but rather to show the reality of some powerful weapons and a tireless friend who promises to help and protect us in the coming battles. More than anything else, I am proclaiming the good news, that God loves us and that it is that love that thrills our hearts, gives life meaning and strengthens us to face the challenges ahead.

> *But those who wait on the LORD shall renew their strength;*
> *They shall mount up with wings like eagles,*
> *They shall run and not be weary,*
> *They shall walk and not faint.*
>
> Isaiah 40:31 NIV

More and more in our secular nation, people hear about Jesus Christ and the Bible but have less and less direct information. For that reason, I would like to present a brief summary of what the Bible tells us and what God through Jesus offers us.

The Bible tells a story of God's love, a relationship broken by mankind's rebellion and selfishness. The Bible interweaves the story of this relationship with the concepts of mankind's free will, faith, judgment, justice, redemption, grace, mercy, forgiveness, and sanctification. Finally and always, the Bible is about God's love. The following is a summary of some major points in that story:

God created mankind and loved us unconditionally. Because we were made in His image, we were meant to love Him back. Love doesn't meant much if it is coerced or programmed in. God gave us free will and, if we love Him, it is of our own free will. As creatures with free will often do, we preferred to be our own bosses, make our own rules and follow our own desires. So we exercised our free will and chose to walk away from God's love and direction. We essentially chose to be our own gods.

Mankind chose selfishness over love of others. We became separated from the knowledge of God's love as we abandoned a relationship with Him. We also became confused as to how we should live. God's love never changed; we just became blind to it. As the history of mankind reveals over and over again, without God's direction, our ways, our desires and choices have inevitably resulted in increasing selfishness, leading to societal disaster, inhumanity and individual human emptiness.

The Bible has a message that *God is love*. God knew that because we had free will and we were not perfect, we would make bad choices at times (Sounds like the kids in the '50s). In His love and mercy, God had a plan from the beginning of time to make a way for mankind to return to His authority, love and care. But first the conflict between mercy and judgment needed to be resolved.

There had to be consequences for our crimes or else a mockery would be made of justice. God Himself chose to solve the dilemma by satisfying justice with His own sacrifice. God came to earth in the form of a man, Jesus Christ, and of His own free will laid down His sinless life to pay the price required by justice for all the unloving acts committed by mankind. In so doing, God made a way for mankind to be restored to a blameless state and therefore to a relationship with Him.

Jesus therefore is called our Redeemer because He paid the price to buy our freedom from bondage to sin and from eternal separation from God.

Mankind did not drag Jesus against His will to the cross. Jesus gave his life freely as a ransom so that we prodigals could return to our Father's presence without the stain of our crimes.

Although it was the sin in us that caused us to crucify Jesus, it was also part of God's plan to use Jesus' sacrifice to show us how much He loves us. The Bible says that Jesus ransomed us by His sacrifice. "Greater love hath no man but that He lay down His life for His friend."

This part of the plan makes sense, as many of us who have kids can imagine how, if a judge sentenced our child to prison or death for his/her crimes, we would choose to take our child's punishment on ourselves rather than watch our kids suffer.

Our part in this agreement is to, by our free will, admit and repent or to turn away from our rebellion and selfish behavior and thoughts. We must also by our free will accept the gift that Jesus paid for and offers to us of forgiveness and reconciliation and resubmit or dedicate ourselves to God's purposes and authority by opening our hearts to Him.

God promises a restoration of our relationship with Him through Christ. For the remainder of our lives the Holy Spirit does the work of "sanctification", or transforming us to be more like Christ-- specifically, more loving. It is this transformation that I call the extreme makeover of the human heart. Then, when we have completed the race, the Holy Spirit will be with us when God calls us home.

We are offered forgiveness, a relationship with the Creator of the Universe, eternal life and the help and guidance of His Spirit in exchange for our repentance and submission. What does God expect of us? Only that we repent and accept Jesus' sacrifice. After the Holy Spirit comes to live inside of us, we should, with His help, do our best to live by His commandments and those are covered by the one, The Golden Rule. What a coincidence that living by the Golden Rule, which is the answer to our nation's problems, is exactly what God has asked of us from the beginning. So why are so many opposed to accepting such a great deal?

Many people reject faith and "religion" because they are leery of the historical excess of "religion" or more specifically, churches. History confirms that many inhumane acts have been committed in the name of God. If we replace the concept of religion with the reality of *the love of God*, it makes what we are seeking clearer. Religion does not free us; God's love does. When we experience God's love inside of us, we are fulfilled and freed. We are free to have a love relationship with the God of the Universe and with one another. "The kingdom of God is loving relationships." That is way beyond religion. It is a mystery and a miracle.

To the extent that people both lived by the Golden Rule and had faith in God in the '50s, life had meaning and people felt connected to each other. Perhaps with the progress made in racial and gender fairness, we could surpass the 1950s watermark and build a nation where we truly have "brotherhood and sisterhood from sea to shining sea."

Others reject God because they reject the idea of sin. Our society today has, via relative values, almost eliminated the concept of "sin". But what is sin, really? According to the Bible, it is breaking God's laws. God Himself says there is one great law that, if obeyed, fulfills all others. This law is the Golden Rule and its companion: "Love the Lord your God with all of your heart soul and mind."

So it is selfishness or breaking the Golden Rule that is sin and it is living by the Golden Rule, or living by love, that fulfills God's commandments. That goes along with the theme of this entire book. It is our selfishness and lack of love that causes us to turn our back on God and our fellow man, and it is this selfishness that has brought our country to ruin.

Others of you reject faith in God because you have questions that are unanswered about life, the Bible, etc., and you are waiting to have all of your questions answered before you sign on the dotted line. But in reality, it is faith that opens the door to getting many of our questions answered, and so waiting and agonizing may be keeping you from getting the very answers you seek.

So when you think you cannot have a relationship with God because of unanswered intellectual questions or disagreements with the Bible or bad feelings about the church, remember, you can't think your way into faith. If you had a neighbor you didn't know much about, would you research everything you could learn about him before you even said hello or would you enter into a relationship with him and expect many of your questions about that neighbor to be answered after you get to know him?

Isaiah 55:9.NKJV: *For as the heavens are higher than the earth, So are My ways higher than your way... And My thoughts than your thoughts.*

After the relationship is restored, when we do talk to God, reach out to Him with our hearts, listen to Him and seek His will through prayer and the Bible, He promises that His Holy Spirit will be inside of us, guiding us and making His presence and will known to us. The choice to accept or reject this gift of forgiveness, love, eternal life and the power of the Holy Spirit is ours.

When you think about it, the steps we take to reunite our hearts with God's are exactly what one would do to restore any friendship damaged by our bad behavior...apologize, take steps to make it right (Jesus did this for us) and make a commitment to making it work in the future.

So what happens when we reaffirm Adam and Eve's position, i.e., that we want to be our own boss, live by our own laws and make our own way in life? God allows us this choice; however, there is a price to be paid. There is a great metaphorical river filled with God's endless, perfect love. This love is there for every individual. It says in the Bible that God's love is always upon us.

> Romans 8:38-39 NIV: *For I am convinced that neither death, nor life, nor angels, nor principalities, nor things present, nor things to come, nor powers, nor height, nor depth, nor any other created thing, will be able to separate us from the love of God.*

However, if we do not have a personal knowledge of God's existence or to put it another way, if we do not personally acknowledge God's existence by accepting the ransom paid by our Savior, Jesus Christ, we are also blocked from the awareness of His love.

For those who would like to get up every day and turn from selfishness and truly love and sacrifice for others but don't know the love of God, it would be wise to connect your hose to that river. In order to do that, we must enter into a relationship with Him through Jesus.

As a final encouragement I want to add this. If you do take this step of faith, you will likely look back, as I have, at the pride and intellectual roadblocks that almost prevented you from experiencing the love and companionship of the Creator of the Universe. Then, like me, you will see how trivial those roadblocks were in comparison with what you have gained.

I have gained among much else, my old childlike heart back that I believed was gone forever. When we connect to the child in ourselves, we are following God's plan as He commands us to "come as a little child." This is not a call to immaturity but to trust, hope, joy, innocence and faith.

> *The Great Man is he who does not lose his childlike heart.*
> Mencius-Samurai Warrior

God is a mighty companion in war and in peace. It's a tough world out there and love can be hard to come by. I never met a person that could sustain and regenerate their love for others each day without a refill somewhere. The Holy Spirit of God sustains us in the face of a world that is upside down in its priorities.

Those who choose can determine to enlist God as a companion in their battles and those who do not wish to are free to continue the struggle without Him. In the end, anyone, believer or non-believer, who chooses to live by the Golden Rule will be furthering our efforts to restore our nation. Consider that perhaps those whose strength lies in the Creator of the universe will have better armor, wiser leadership, clearer direction and more endurance and greater joy in the battle. We are, as humans, a little puny.

Do you want to experience the love of God, be given the strength to truly love and sacrifice for others, to know that you are forgiven of your selfish behaviors, have eternal life in heaven, and have the help and guidance of the Spirit of God every day of your life here on Earth? Then submit yourself to Him by saying the following prayer with all of the sincerity that is in your heart.

Lord, I come before you as a sinner. I know my selfishness has caused me to sin over and over again and I am sorry. Please forgive me and help me to change. Thank you, Lord Jesus, for sacrificing yourself, out of your Love for me, and paying the price demanded by Justice for my sins. I ask you according to your Word to come in Your Spirit and live inside of me and be my Lord and Savior. Please change me to be the unselfish loving person that You want me to be. Thank you for granting me eternal life and for your Holy Spirit. Show me how to live according to the purpose and plans you have for me.

If, by your will and heart you have chosen to take this step of faith, the Bible says that through grace (the free gift of God) you are forgiven and you are destined for eternal life. In addition, in this world the door is now open for you to resume a direct relationship with God through Jesus and through the presence of His Holy Spirit, who is now living inside of you. The Bible says that all of Heaven and all of the angels celebrate when one lost soul comes home. You are the reason Heaven is celebrating today.

CHAPTER 45

As We Go Forward

Now, we are an army of individuals who love our nation and its people. Some of us have had an extreme makeover of our hearts. Others are offering themselves in their own strength. Our agenda is to love one another, serve one another and in so doing, "preserve the blessings of freedom to ourselves and our posterity."

In order to avoid as much as possible the pitfalls of the '60s, we must have a leader who will not veer off course or grow too tired, angry or cynical to do what is right. We must have a leader who knows right from wrong and who has an understanding of and patience with human weakness. Most of all, we need a leader who has an endless love for people and whose decisions and actions are motivated by that love.

God's Holy Spirit is the only leader who can lead us past the pitfalls of human weakness and keep us on the right course. The best news is that God has promised Him to us when we accept Jesus' sacrifice and return to God (John 14:16-18 NIV):

And I will ask the Father, and he will give you another Counselor to be with you forever—the Spirit of truth. The world cannot accept him, because it neither sees him nor knows him. But you know him, for he lives with you and will be in you.

With God's Spirit leading the way we will not pollute the ends by using unethical means. When we treat others as we would want to be treated, our efforts and sacrifices will be multiplied and grow, rather than be diminished by the corruption and self-serving scheming that is so common today. There will be a domino effect of decency, honesty and caring that will hopefully see us through the end of the age.

God, though His Holy Spirit will guide us into all wisdom and will keep us from compromising the ends with the wrong means as we did in the '60s. He will keep us from jealousies, greed, and a desire for power, recognition and revenge. Above all, He will sustain us in the midst of the hatred and evil that men do.

In the 1960s we did not invite God to be our leader. The Bible tells us to put on the full armor of God before we go into battle:

Therefore put on the full armor of God, so that when the day of evil comes, you may be able to stand your ground, and after you have done everything, to stand. [14] *Stand firm then, with the belt of truth buckled around your waist, with the breastplate of righteousness in place,* [15] *and with your feet fitted with the readiness that comes from the gospel of peace.* [16] *In addition to all this, take up the shield of faith, with which you can extinguish all the flaming arrows of the evil one.* [17] *Take the helmet of salvation and the sword of the Spirit, which is the word of God. NIV*

Ephesians 6:13-18, NIV.

If we consult the Holy Spirit each day for our marching orders, let Him guide us in every situation and get used to looking to Him for wisdom and strength, we will not stray from the path God has planned.

Today, those who understand must do what we can to make sure that what comes is love, not hate, and giving, not taking. We will undoubtedly have losses. We will also have gains. If we lose some or even most of our economic prosperity, it does not mean that we can't be happy. There is much in terms of human relationships that we have lost, and we now have the opportunity to have those relationships restored out of necessity. We must learn again how to depend on each other and help each other. The joy of truly giving and caring about others again and the meaning and purpose that knowing God provides will overcome the fear and will provide the hope we are all desperately looking for.

However, what is unacceptable is the loss of our freedoms. We must fight against that with every weapon that God gives us. If we do not compromise our mission and if the means we use are motivated by love then, no matter what comes, we are and will be free.

When we are opposed, by those whose agenda includes our bondage to their tyranny, we must turn away from them and focus on our leader, The Holy Spirit of God. We must live as He wants us to live regardless of what the powers of this world are doing. To defeat us they must control us and to do that they must get our attention.

CHAPTER 46

A Message to the Younger Generation

At this point, I would like to offer a special challenge to those young people who have reached out in faith and returned to God. You are among a small but growing number of your generation who have come up out of the confusion and darkness of the selfish world into the light of love, purpose and truth. That may sound hokey, but think for a minute about what it means. Love (the only thing in this life that fulfills us eternally), purpose (love's motivation to get up and look forward to every day) and truth (that reality which is real, wisdom)....and the TRUTH will set you free.

As you walk on your God-directed path, do not forget those of your generation who are still lost. It is your great challenge and privilege to re-enter the dark world with the power of the Holy Spirit shining through you and show many the way out. Perhaps you have friends or family members who do not know the love of God. Consider talking to them, taking them to church or sharing what God is doing for you.

Even though you may not know it yet, you have made a decision that will change your life forever. If you allow God's Holy Spirit to lead you, every day can be filled with new discoveries about the wonderful complexity and potential of human beings. I know what I'm talking about when I say that all the money, power and fame in the world cannot come close to equaling the satisfaction, excitement and purpose you will find in a life lived, by the power of God, in such a way as to motivate others to follow the same path that you have just chosen.

Our nation is in trouble. We need everyone to join in the struggle to bring the United States back to God and through God to brotherhood, honesty, kindness, patience, forgiveness, perseverance, long-suffering, kindness and love. We need you to care enough to give of your time, energy and voice to "pay forward" the love that God gives you to others. There is no greater calling than this.

---------- CHAPTER 47 ----------

A Message for the Baby Boomers

I also have a message for my generation, the baby boomers. I have at times been pretty hard on our generation. We have been arrogant and thoughtless when it comes to honoring the things of God, and we have often been selfish in our actions toward each other. But we are also the generation who once believed in sacrificing for others, being fair and telling it like it was.... or at least how we believed it was. Some of our ideals were naïve and ill-conceived from the start and others were solid, altruistic hopes that we let slip from our hands as circumstances changed and we became more callous.

On our behalf, there is much to be said for those who, rather than sit back and tolerate an intolerable status quo, would risk everything to promote what we believed was a just cause. Besides, without the missing ingredient, God's love and Spirit inside of us, we were doomed by our own selfish nature in our attempt to implement the idealistic agenda of peace, love and harmony among all people.

The majority of the baby boomers long ago abandoned our optimistic dedication to making a positive difference in our world. As we approach the "winter" of our lives, we like generations before us, are increasingly aware of our own mortality as well as the accompanying questions of purpose and meaning in our lives. Many of us aren't so sure we ever found it.

Once again, humanity stands at a critical crossroads and we again have the opportunity to have a positive impact on the world and our country for ourselves and future generations. It is time to admit to our mistakes and face the dead end that our arrogance, our worship of selfishness and our abandonment of God have led us to and do a you-turn and go in another direction. We owe it to the upcoming generations to do this.

With the power of our Creator energizing, renewing and guiding us, the innovation, optimism and altruism which were once the hallmark of our generation will be utilized in furthering the message of God's love to each and every person. As we work side by side with our children and grandchildren to build a better community, country and world, I believe the purpose and meaning of our lives will become clear. For many of us it will also be a trip home, to the values and faith we were brought up with.

Therefore we also, since we are surrounded by so great a cloud of witnesses, let us lay aside every weight, and the sin which so easily ensnares us, and let us run with endurance the race that is set before us, [2] looking unto Jesus, the author and finisher of our faith, who for the joy that was set before Him endured the cross, despising the shame, and has sat down at the right hand of the throne of God. Hebrews 12:1-2, NKJV.

Let us lay aside the weights of arrogance, fear, regret, pride, envy, greed and anger and dedicate ourselves to living according to God's law: to love one another as we love ourselves. Then, when we have finished the race, history may record that the baby boomers went out with a "boom" instead of "sitting around talking about glory days" or watching someone else's life on a reality show.

Perhaps posterity will add a last act to the *Big Chill*. This will be the scene in which we boomers lift our heads and look each other, our children and ourselves in the eyes, knowing that although we made some wrong turns, with God's help, we finished the race on course.

JFK said, "To whom much is given, much is expected." The baby boom generation has been given much--by our parents, by our country and by our God. If we finish this race as God intends, we will have finally fulfilled, with God's help, the promise we made as a generation over 50 years ago to leave this country and world a better, more loving place for the generation(s) behind us.

www.ingramcontent.com/pod-product-compliance
Lightning Source LLC
Chambersburg PA
CBHW020416290526
45785CB00002B/585